Building Community

Answering Kennedy's Call

Building Community

Answering Kennedy's Call

Harlan Russell Green

A PEACE CORPS WRITERS BOOK

Building Community

Answering Kennedy's Call

ISBN-13: 978-1-950444-41-0

Library of Congress Control Number: 2022905345

First Peace Corps Writers Edition, April 2022

I dedicate this book to all who
have volunteered to make the
world a better place to live.

Building Community
Answering Kennedy's Call

TABLE OF CONTENTS

Preface

I began writing this memoir about my work in public service in 2017, after wondering how it was possible that Americans had elected a president suffering a severe mental disorder. Did it mean our democracy was dying or already dead, and Americans now wanted a demagogue as president who believed that he was above all laws and the constitution?

It reminded me in many ways of the 1960s when there was just as much social unrest and different ideas of democracy. This was the era of McCarthyism and communist witch-hunting, right wing against left wing political views, the civil rights movement, and an unpopular war in Vietnam that was fracturing American communities.

We coped with the dysfunction and cynicism then by searching for communities that could mirror our values and ideals, and when we found them, to contribute to their growth.

I am writing about my years working to develop successful communities to show that it is possible to do it today in the face of so much social unrest that has created deep divisions and the possibility of future wars.

I believe that spirit of service is alive in younger generations that also want to make their country a better place. Many of them in the Millennial and Generation Z population groups are also searching for like-minded communities that serve a greater cause, that will bring people together in common purpose rather than separate them.

The Peace Corps was such a cause I believed in. I became a Peace Corps Volunteer to work in a program that improved the lives of Turkish farmworkers. A few years later I joined the Environmental Protection Agency at its inception because it was an organization dedicated to protecting the environment with the newly enacted Clean Water and Air Acts.

My membership in the United Farmworkers Union under César Chávez later in the mid-1970s was more happenstance. A cousin of mine in the construction trades roped me into helping him rebuild the UFW's new headquarters, and it was extremely difficult to withstand the charisma of its founder and president, César Chávez. I was soon swept up in his vision of a union formed to improve the working conditions of Mexican farmworkers.

These were organizations dedicated to improving lives that taught me the fundamentals of healthy communities, fundamentals that enabled me to continue to improve the lives in my own community and led to the formation of a new California city.

There were many others doing what I did in that era. My history is one small part of the change that has been happening in American communities, towns, and cities whose members seek to improve their lives.

Former President Obama challenged Americans to inspire the youth to a life of service in 2017 after he left the presidency; and the youth he talked about are my target audience. He said then:

> We have some of the lowest voting rates of any democracy and low participation rates that translate into a further gap between who's governing us and what we believe. The only folks who are going to be able to solve that problem are going to be young people, the next generation. And I have been encouraged everywhere I go in the United States, but also everywhere around the world to see how sharp and astute and tolerant and thoughtful and entrepreneurial our young people are. A lot more sophisticated than I was at their age. And so the question then becomes what are the ways in which we can create pathways for them to take leadership, for them to get involved?[1]

President Obama's words came from his experience as a community organizer in Chicago. And studies show that Millennials and Generation Z youth now reaching adulthood want to make the world they have inherited a better place to live. Millennials' preferences will be influential for no other reason than they are the largest generation ever, born from 1980

---

[1] http://thehill.com/blogs/pundits-blog/the-administration/330269-full- re-marks-obama-at-chicago-event-discusses-future

to 1996, outnumbering even their Baby Boomer parents. They are also a much more diverse and tolerant population, which is why they are picking up where we left off in their preference for making worthwhile life choices.

"Almost two-thirds (64 percent) of Millennials said they would rather make $40,000 a year at a job they love than $100,000 a year at a job they think is boring," the Brookings Institution recently noted in a report by Morley Winograd and Michael Hais titled "How Millennials Could Upend Wall Street and Corporate America."[2]

It cites a 2013 survey of over 1,200 U.S. adults that found Millennials to be the generation most focused on corporate social responsibility when making purchasing decisions. Almost all Millennials responded with increased trust (91 percent) and loyalty (89 percent), as well as a stronger likelihood to buy from those companies that supported solutions to specific social issues (89 percent). A majority of Millennials reported buying a product that had a social benefit, and 84 percent of a generation that accounts for more than $1 trillion in U.S. consumer spending considered a company's involvement in social causes in deciding what to buy or where to shop. In 2013, 89 percent of all American consumers said they would consider switching brands to one associated with a good cause if price and quality were equal.

One 30-year-old Millennial said in 2013, the 50th anniversary of President Kennedy's death, that

---

[2] https://www.brookings.edu/wp- content/uploads/2016/06/Brookings_
Winogradfinal.pdf

Though his [Kennedy's] goals were typically big, what he sought from individuals was often rather small. Not everyone was expected to join the Peace Corps or become an astronaut or participate in the Freedom Rides. But citizens were asked to do their part—to think about how they could improve their community or make another person's life easier—to look past their differences and focus on our common humanity. We badly need this message again. I believe it is one that resonates deeply with young Americans who are yearning for a time when we can search for new frontiers and once again be part of the same team.[3]

The Kennedy Era

The Peace Corps is just one aspect of our government's effort to practice the elements needed to build and strengthen peaceful communities in developing countries. There are many other so-called NGOs—non-governmental organizations—that serve in other countries, and AmeriCorps functions in a similar way in American cities to boost opportunities of the under-served.

The Peace Corps has been a success in large part because Sargent Shriver, JFK's brother-in-law, the first Director of the Peace Corps and many Great Society programs, inspired us with his call to "Service above Self", serving something greater than

---

[3] https://www.huffingtonpost.com/scott-d-reich/jfk-millennials_b_4263057.html

oneself that would be needed to create a more peaceful and just world.

This dedication to service was promoted in President Kennedy's acceptance speech at the 1960 Democratic National convention, when he said

> We stand today on the edge of a New Frontier
> —the frontier of the 1960s, the frontier of
> unknown opportunities and perils, the frontier of
> unfilled hopes and unfilled threats . . . Beyond
> that frontier are uncharted areas of science
> and space, unsolved problems of peace and
> war, unconquered problems of ignorance and
> prejudice, unanswered questions of poverty and
> surplus.

His was the defining presidency of the sixties that moved many of my generation with his message of new possibilities because he saw the need for models of change in a world still fighting the Cold War while recovering from a world war.

The U.S. Peace Corps was one of Kennedy's first creations, but he also benefited America's poorest and seniors by signing social legislation raising the minimum wage and increasing Social Security benefits. He also supported Martin Luther King, Jr.'s call for greater justice for African Americans by supporting James Meredith's attempt to enroll at the University of Mississippi and ordering his Attorney General, brother Bobby Kennedy, to protect the Freedom Riders in the South.

This book recognizes the many ways such a spirit of service is restoring communities and hope for a better future. It describes the sense of community and common purpose that prevailed in the early decades of post-World War II America that I lived through.

I hope it provides a useful measure of what is needed to restore our faith in democracy imperiled by the rise of authoritarian governments, global pandemics, and a warming planet.

All things are possible with the spirit and mind-set that enables one to serve causes that better the lives of others, as opposed to the "me first" narcissism so prevalent in much of American culture today.

Chapter One

The Call to Serve

It was the morning of November 22, 1963, a moment that I and many others say they remember with startling clarity.

I was among a group of University of California, Berkeley students crowded around a black and white television in the lobby of the new Student Union when we heard that President Kennedy had been shot while in a caravan parading through Dallas, Texas.

Kennedy was in Dallas to raise money for his re-election campaign and bring together liberal and conservative factions in the state Democratic Party. Freedom Riders, civil rights marchers and Ku Klux Klan rallies had made Dallas and the southern states a dangerous place for social activists. He was scheduled to speak to local leaders at a luncheon at the Dallas Business and Trade Mart that day.

We hoped that President Kennedy would survive, only to watch Walter Cronkite announce he had died at 1 pm, Dallas time.

There was shocked silence and muffled sobbing at Berkeley, all part of a moment that seemed to last an eternity.

We streamed outside into what I remember as a bright day and a changed world. A surreally bright sunlight bathed UC's Sproul Plaza filled with groups of students in conversation as the news quickly spread of President Kennedy's death.

At the bottom of the Student Union steps was a Peace Corps recruiting table with two serious looking recruiters talking to no one in particular, the papers in front of them ruffled by a slight breeze. They looked as shocked as I was at the news of Kennedy's death.

I knew little about the Peace Corps: there was a possibility of draft deferment from military service if accepted as a volunteer, and it probably meant living in primitive conditions.

The developing world was a place where poverty was pervasive, though I knew nothing about the conditions that caused it. I was more interested in learning about cultures outside of an America still mired in a Cold War crusade from the McCarthy era, than with America's take-it-or-leave-it history with countries that did not mirror our system of government.

I volunteered for the Peace Corps on that day because I wanted to answer his call, as many others did, to "Ask not what your country can do for you, ask what you can do for your country."

The University Environment

The University of California, Berkeley campus in 1968 had fewer students and more green space when I enrolled as a freshman, more space for students to congregate or study. I had no idea it was an ideal place to spawn student protests like the free speech movement and anti-war demonstrations when I enrolled.

There was a huge lawn in front of the Men's Gym. There were several beautiful eucalyptus groves to wander through on our way to classes that gave the illusion that we were distant from the noisy city that surrounded the campus.

Berkeley and the East Bay in the early sixties were not the home of street people or war protestors. We had to visit San Francisco's coffee houses to hear Beat poets like Jack Kerouac and Lawrence Ferlinghetti call for free love, pot smoking and rebelling against an old order.

Berkeley had just a few coffee houses where we discussed segregation, job discrimination, and civil rights. The Mediterranean Café on Telegraph Avenue served Italian coffees and my favorite, Granita, a terrific frozen coffee desert.

The UC campus did have a Greek Amphitheatre, where I attended a production of *Lysistrata*, maybe the first anti-war play, by Aristophanes written during Athens's incessant wars (431 to 405 B.C.E.) with the neighboring city of Sparta.

Lysistrata was about the women of Athens who had grown tired of their men's constant warring and decided to ban sex with them until they sued for peace. We in the audience streamed into the central arena after the performance and tasted samples of Australian Brandy put out by the Australian cast while we discussed Aristophanes's take on the Peloponnesian wars.

It was an example of the anti-war discussions of those early days. We knew almost nothing about an ongoing civil war in Vietnam until publication of *The Ugly American* by two Berkeley Associate Professors in 1958, my freshman year.

I attended their lecture on campus at the book's publication. It created a tremendous debate in Berkeley at a time when few of us were even aware of what was happening in Vietnam.

Edgar Snow also lectured about his book *Red Star Over China* that described his journey with Mao Zedong on the long march to win China's civil war and how the US had taken sides on their civil war; and I heard Malcom X speak on campus about why African Americans needed a country of their own to find true freedom.

It was hard to notice what was happening in this mesmerizingly beautiful campus with its Memorial Stadium that held up to 100,000 football fans of UC's Golden Bears and the beautiful, wooded slope above it called Strawberry Canyon that led up to Lawrence Laboratory and the Cyclotron, one of the first atom-splitting particle accelerators.

Vietnam

We began to hear talk about a possible war in Vietnam in 1964, my senior year. There had been a third military coup and President Johnson was promising military aid to South Vietnam.

The Ugly American had described the misguided attempts of American diplomats and foreign aid workers to help the South Vietnamese in their war with North Vietnam.

It portrayed the death and destruction in the country that had just driven out the French colonial occupiers at the battle of Dienbienphu. The book was later released as a movie with Marlon Brando starring as an arrogant, pipe-smoking ambassador who wanted to bring the American idea of progress to Vietnam amid its civil war.

President Kennedy was said to have given a copy of the novel to every U.S. Senator, and that it gave him the idea to form the Peace Corps.

Professors Lederer and Burdick's words influenced many of us at that time. How could President Johnson be ignorant about what was going on in Vietnam and the rest of Asia, for that matter? The French had lost Vietnam for a reason. The Vietnamese did not want us there, I thought. Why were we any different than the French?

Vietnam was never mentioned as other than a small civil war with South Vietnam being supported by so-called Green Berets and the CIA until my senior year.

Acceptance into the Peace Corps

There were not many choices for my future at the time. There was the military and maybe Vietnam if we became more involved, or escaping to Canada, or service in the Peace Corps in an unknown land.

I volunteered for the Peace Corps because I believed President Kennedy was serious about finding more peaceful solutions to our problems. I had heard him speak while a student at UC Berkeley. He spoke on March 23, 1962, to commemorate the 94th anniversary of the University of California's founding, the year before he was assassinated. We were 77,000 students packed in UC Berkeley's Memorial Stadium to hear President Kennedy.

We wanted to know what our future might look like because Russia was still threatening nuclear war. A civil war in Vietnam was in the news, and Americans were already involved, but many of us opposed military service. We wanted to believe in Kennedy's vision that the Cold War with Russia could end peacefully.

President Kennedy said on that day:

> . . . a cooperative Soviet-American effort in space science and exploration would emphasize the interests that must unite us, rather than those that always divide us. It offers us an area in which the stale and sterile dogmas of the Cold War could be literally left a quarter of a million miles behind. And it would remind us on both sides that knowledge, not hate, is the passkey to the future—that knowledge transcends national antagonisms—that it speaks a universal language—that it is the possession, not of a single class, or of a single nation or a single ideology, but of all mankind.[1]

---

[1] https://www.jfklibrary.org/archives/other-resources/john-f-kennedy-speeches/university-of-california-berkeley-19620323

JFK gave us the picture of a new future, promising a peaceful settlement to the Cold War, of scientific research and alternatives for peaceful service that could benefit all nations. His speech gave me hope that the world could become a better place than living under the continual fear of war that I had experienced since elementary school hunkered under a desk with every civil defense drill. Many friends and colleagues have said they experienced the same "aha" moment on hearing Kennedy speak, and that it could be their life's work.

Even though I had volunteered, a draft notice arrived from my Selective Service Board that senior year after I had also passed a physical exam by Army doctors. There had been no word from the Peace Corps regarding my acceptance to be a Volunteer, or indication my Draft Board might grant a deferment if I was accepted.

Then, just in time, one month before June graduation when I was scheduled to report for military service, word came from the Peace Corps of my acceptance; I was to serve in Turkey for two years. My hometown draft board gave me a one-year deferment. They wished me well as a Peace Corps Volunteer and stated that a deferment might be extended for a second year, pending a letter from wherever I was serving.

It was a close call. I had no desire to join the military. It was the face of America I did not want to see or represent. I had heard too many stories of CIA-led uprisings that overthrew countries like Iran (whose Prime Minister was threatening to nationalize the Anglo-Iranian oil fields) and was up to no good in Vietnam.

15

What followed was the opportunity to serve two very eventful years in Turkey helping farmers in a rural community development program.

That was the beginning of my years of public service, a calling I believe is even more important today in building back a more peaceful world that is threatened by foreign and domestic terrorism, mass migrations, inequality, and racial bigotry.

Chapter Two

Boot Camp for a Peace Corps Volunteer

My life as a Peace Corps Volunteer began on August 10, 1964, just days after the U.S. declared war on North Vietnam. President Johnson signed the Gulf of Tonkin Resolution as I was in training to become a Peace Corps Volunteer serving in the country of Turkey—a contrast that haunted me through most of the next two years. We were to serve while living and working in Turkish villages, where we were expected to aid in their economic development.

The training site in lush, beautiful Vermont was Rudyard Kipling's former American estate, Sandanona, where he wrote the *Jungle Books*. It had become the Experiment in International Living, a training site for exchange students and teachers that Peace Corps chose for our three months of training. The campus consisted of a group of white bungalows clustered around an algae-filled swimming pool, several volleyball courts, and a language laboratory where we would spend four hours per day, six days a week attempting to learn the Turkish language.

We were assisted by ten Turkish language teachers imported from Istanbul for the first six weeks. They taught us enough

Turkish to (perhaps) enable us to survive and thrive in remote Turkish villages where little, if any, English was spoken.

Mustafa Kemal Ataturk was Turkey's "George Washington", an Army General who had founded the Turkish Republic. He modernized the Turkish alphabet from the original Arabic script by converting it to 29 Roman letters. It made the printed words easier to learn. We were told that no more than six hundred words were needed to have an ordinary conversation in Turkish. Could speaking an unfamiliar foreign language create friendships as well as bring new ideas to Turkey's very conservative villages?

The surrounding, jungle-like Vermont forest was a steamy 90-100 degrees that August, which could have caused Kipling to feel he was still in India when he wrote about Mowgli and his jungle creatures. I was bowled over to be in the middle of such a place. Sandanona's history helped to reinforce the spirit of adventure I was already feeling. We were gathered in one place that was already a part of history, in training to serve as volunteers making history in Turkey: the first volunteers to live and work in Muslim villages. Service in a Turkish village where seasons were more important than the 24-hour day would be a challenge, but I was excited at being part of an historical event. Our Peace Corps group would be the first to bridge the wide divide between eastern and western cultures and religions in a Muslim countryside where most Turks still lived at the time. I hoped I could contribute to a developing country that, according to the Turkish government, was 99 percent Muslim.

Our Indoctrination

First came our indoctrination by the State Department and scholars on why the Peace Corps was working in Third World countries. President Kennedy created the Peace Corps in 1961 to "promote world peace and friendship" through three goals: (1) to help the peoples of interested countries in meeting their need for trained men and women; (2) to help promote a better understanding of Americans on the part of the peoples served; and (3) to help promote a better understanding of other peoples on the part of Americans.

Kennedy chose his brother-in-law Sargent Shriver to be Peace Corps's first director because Shriver was a man of high ideals and an incredible work ethic. Shriver's early remarks and inspirational speeches, especially his call to "Service above Self" as the highest ideal of any human endeavor, gave meaning to my two years of service. He once said in an interview that

> Peace Corps Volunteers . . . have come to realize
> . . . that the world is a real community. They have
> learned that people can cross barriers of language
> and culture and customs. They've learned foreign
> languages, yes, but more important they have
> learned to hear the voice of the human heart in
> any language.

There were plenty of critics on the political right and left who saw no immediate benefit from sending Americans to live in primitive places. Shriver described some of the criticisms in a 1986 speech to returned Peace Corps Volunteers:

Conservatives opposed the word "Peace"! They maintained it sounded wishy-washy, vague, and weak. The Communists, they said, had corrupted the word "Peace" by applying it to every political initiative, and even to every war they got involved in.

The left-wing disliked the word "Corps"! They said it sounded militaristic. The famous "German Afrika Corps", victorious almost everywhere under General Rommel, was fresh in their minds. "Corps" sounded like a scourge . . .

By the end of 1963, 7,000 volunteers were serving in 44 Third World countries. Peace Corps enrollment peaked in 1966 with more than 15,000 volunteers in 52 countries. Since 1961, more than 200,000 Americans have joined the Peace Corps, serving in 134 nations—including eastern Europe, Russia (briefly), Mongolia and China.

Our Mission

The Peace Corps was still unknown to most Americans when 77 of us began training to live in mostly remote Turkish villages. This was a part of the world most of us knew nothing about.

I wanted to learn how others lived, even learn new ways I might live if I survived the grueling selection process. A psychologist and psychiatrist were on the staff. Peace Corps wanted to know if we had the mental fortitude to endure the primitive living conditions of age-old Muslim villages, many isolated in the winter and without much support.

We might live and work in a Turkish village without electricity or the basic sanitary facilities that Americans were used to.

We had to learn not only their language, but also the Turkish culture if we were to be accepted as credible and effective helpers to Turkish villagers who wanted to boost their standard of living.

We might need to help villagers find good drinking water, irrigation water to grow their crops, perhaps even better kinds of crops and livestock that would be more successful. Female volunteers would work and advise on health issues and in women's vocational education classes, where they existed. Those were our assignments, at least. Peace Corps training at that time was still a work in process.

In learning about the history of Turkey, I was curious to know more about the "terrible Turk" warrior reputation acquired during and after the Ottoman Empire. It was a study in contrasts. The Turks' brutality during the Armenian massacre and Long March in 1915 may have killed 500,000 Armenians. On the other hand, their bravery while participating in the Korean War saved many Allied lives. I wanted to understand how a country with such a warrior tradition had become a republic modeled after western democracies.

Learning Community Building

When I was young, I had worked with my hands doing projects in our one-acre back yard with my dad, one of which included hand-drilling a water well with a posthole auger (knowledge that helped me in Turkey when searching for irrigation water). We raised rabbits and chickens, and even traded for fresh milk over the fence with a neighbor who had a cow. It gave me a sense of what I might encounter in a Turkish farming community. I had also worked as a union carpenter during summers to earn money for UC Berkeley. These skills would be helpful, but three months was hardly enough to acquire all the skills needed to live and work in a Turkish village.

We were told we would be taught the concept of community development by government aid workers. This meant learning how to encourage Turkish farmers to try more modern methods of agriculture and to learn other skills they might want or need.

I knew nothing about community development or community organizing, and little about their agricultural techniques that had been used for centuries. But we were assured we could learn and import knowledge from experts back home or consult Turkish government ministries that might also be of help.

It really meant I would be functioning as a facilitator rather than an expert. That was my rudimentary understanding of community development at the time.

From eight in the morning to ten at night, six days a week, we were lectured, indoctrinated, and given language training so intense that some of the recruits began to drop out. The lectures included subjects we needed to know about for personal safety: from dealing with rabies to 15-foot long Ascaris (tape) worms in our intestines, to so-called canine ulcers from parasites in uncooked vegetables that could grow in our bodies and poison us up to ten years later if they burst. Staff also warned of the physical dangers surviving severe winters in remote mountains of eastern Turkey where volunteers could be snowed in for months in villages only accessible via foot path at that time. We were even warned where it was safe to sit in public transportation, especially during the severe winter weather that prevailed at that latitude and higher elevation of the Anatolian Plateau, which rose to 6,000 feet in parts of eastern Turkey.

We were warned of the political dangers in a country that had struggled with two military coups since the 1950s. It did not seem like such a big deal to me after six years enduring Berkeley's politics, but State Department officials wanted us to know that Turkey was a veritable cauldron of political protests.

We were cautioned against participating in demonstrations in cities where many of our friends and associates would be teaching in Turkish schools and universities, and where student demonstrations could be as spontaneous as in Berkeley. But really, I thought, how political could it get in a Turkish village?

We spent six more weeks of training in the Vermont countryside outside of the small town of Calais, just north of Vermont's capital, Montpelier, and less than one day's drive from the Canadian border and Quebec.

It was a part of Vermont that was off the beaten path. Descendants of pioneer families still lived on farms that dated from the 1700s. Our training mission was to assist the Calais locals in restoring some historical sites to create a museum.

We camped in large tents in a farmer's meadow to learn the ways of rural Vermonters. We rebuilt stone walls with a Vermont stone mason, repaired a country road, constructed a septic tank, and learned cooking and housekeeping methods that the female volunteers might encounter in Turkish villages.

Several of us with enough manual skills were given the task of restoring Vermont's longest running water-powered sawmill that had stopped working years before.

The Robinson Sawmill was built in 1803 and had been cutting logs into planks until the late 1950s. The two ponds that provided water for the mill silted up enough that it could only be run during the winter rainy season. But now the East Calais Historical Society wanted it rebuilt to be part of their historical museum.

The sawmill was powered by the earliest power source— water flowing over a 20-foot-high dam. The flow had enough pressure funneled through a large diameter penstock to spin a turbine at the bottom. The turbine then turned rotating shafts that powered the immense sawblade.

The turbine's timber housing had rotted and needed to be rebuilt along with the shed's rock foundation. This was a problem that several of us with a carpentry background knew how to fix.

It was a grand historical occasion and a wonder to behold when the 80-year-old sawyer of the original mill once again was able to cut logs. It still runs today after a second restoration under the auspices of the Aldrich Memorial Association, Inc.

of Calais, Vermont, a charitable foundation set up to keep the sawmill running.

What Were We Volunteering for?

Men and women were segregated in Muslim villages, which tended to be more conservative in their religious practices. Two-thirds of our trainees were married couples to better work with both sexes. However, since males could only work with the village men on projects and volunteer females could work only with the village women, each of us who were single were paired with a compatible partner of the opposite sex.

The Peace Corps training staff was looking for volunteers who embodied a certain optimism, an enthusiastic state of mind we would need to keep our spirits up when in the more primitive environment we would likely find in Turkish villages.

The staff seemed to be concerned about our attitude towards homosexuality, for instance. We would be living in Turkish villages with only intermittent contact with Peace Corps officials and other volunteers. Turkey had a strict social code preventing casual male and female social companionship. But behavior was more uninhibited in showing friendships within their own genders. It therefore was not unusual for male friends to hold hands as they were strolling and conversing.

I made a point of telling our staff psychiatrist and psychologist I had no problem with showing male affection. I knew showing any discomfort over the issue of male homosexuality in Turkey could set off alarm bells with staff concerned about emotional stability. Even so, I was one of a small group taken to the Brattleboro State Hospital for various psychological tests.

Male volunteers were issued condoms to protect against venereal diseases, since prostitution was legal in Turkey and who knows what single young American men might do when exposed to what was in some ways a more permissive culture? We were told we should behave as Turks did with the sexes separated, which meant to act conservatively, especially in the more religious countryside. As rural community developers, we were Westerners required to live in an Asian culture where conformity was the norm to avoid any conflict, where it was sometimes easier for our hosts to say "yes" to please a young American, making it difficult to know what behavior was appropriate.

Forty-six of the 77 recruits remained after the harrowing selection process, and many of those who remained did not last two years. In total, 40 percent of the fifth Peace Corps group recruited to serve in Turkey were either not selected during training or dropped out during those two years.

Chapter Three

Survival in a Turkish Village

Travelers and tourists in Turkey today would not recognize Turkey of the 1960s. There were few airports and hotels outside of the largest cities. One had to take a ferry to cross the Bosporus Strait between Europe and Asia rather than the suspension bridges that exist today. Many of the ancient antiquities of Greece and Rome that tourists liked to visit couldn't be reached during winters due to poor roads and harsh weather. Most of the villages we volunteers worked in had no paved roads and few had electricity.

We flew to Turkey in November. I still have a newspaper photo of our volunteer group being greeted by then Prime Minister Ismet Inonu when we first arrived in Turkey. It was a humbling experience being greeted by the Prime Minister who was also Ataturk's commanding general when the Turkish Army fought off the Greek Army invasion in the 1920s, just before the modern Turkish Republic was formed. Prime Minister Inonu was now 80 years old, a tall and very thin gentleman with a hearing aid dangling from one ear. I thought being introduced to the Turkish Prime Minister was a sign the Turkish government welcomed and approved of Peace Corps Volunteers wanting to better the living conditions of Turkish villagers.

Who Were We?

My Peace Corps group came from all parts of our country with a high level of manual skills and practical work experience. Peace Corps selected us for our versatility and adaptability. Our group included nurses, teachers, engineers, carpenters, laborers, a mechanic, a lumberjack, ranch hand, deck hand, governess, bartender, migrant minister, two postal workers, several social workers and one army veteran.

Newly-weds Nikos and Rhonda were the two I most admired because they had studied at the American University in Cairo, Egypt. Their familiarity with the Middle East made them a font of information about Islamic customs and history. They were assigned to a remote village near the Sea of Marmara that had no road, just a path to the outside world. Timber-cutting and woodworking were its main industries. The Turkish Ministry of Agriculture wanted to know if the villagers could learn better methods of harvesting and marketing forestry products.

Betty was a single, middle-aged nurse from Kansas assigned to work in a small day care center in the Ankara ghetto. The ghetto was called a *Gecekondo*, which in Turkish literally meant a dwelling constructed overnight and made of whatever materials were at hand, usually with a corrugated metal roof and cardboard or plywood walls. There were one million inhabitants in this ghetto housing, populated by the most recent arrivals from villages at the time. The housing sprang up to avoid the official red tape and building laws required for legal housing.

The female village volunteers had the most difficult time because they lived within the restrictions placed on Turkish women living in rural areas. The volunteers were required to cover their head and most of their body in public, and to behave as modestly as Islamic women. Religious practices were more conservative in the countryside making their jobs more difficult and causing some to leave early.

Ned and Julie, a married couple, had perhaps the most hair-raising experience living in a remote village in the mountains of western Turkey that became totally isolated after some monster winter storms. They had to survive on rice and beans for several months because there was no access to the nearest market towns for other food during that time. Ned lost 59 pounds. Their isolation was finally broken with the spring thaw.

The villagers proudly donated a live chicken to vary their diet. In a hurry to eat it, Ned sawed off its head with a dull hacksaw rather than using a method he had learned during training—a sharp jab into its mouth with a knife that would kill it instantly to keep the meat tender. Their first meal celebrating the breaking of their isolation was to eat a chicken as tough as leather.

Another couple lived less than 100 kilometers from Pergamum, a fabled Greek and Roman city on the Aegean coast. Their village had not developed a drinking water system beyond hand-dug wells, a common problem in my village and many other villages in our group. Yet many of the ancient Greek and

Roman cities surrounding it had both municipal water and sewer systems more than 2,000 years earlier.

The Peace Corps Volunteers from our group nearest to our village were a two-hour bus ride up an extremely narrow, rock-cliff canyon into mountains and forests. It was an extremely poor village with a high infant mortality rate. During the seemingly endless, snowbound winters—sometimes lasting six months—nursing mothers would run out of milk due to inadequate nutrition. The female volunteer had been a nurse, so she was able to show the mothers how to provide nutritional supplements to their diet.

It was the beginning of winter and already cold when we arrived. Istanbul, Turkey's largest city, is at the same latitude as Boston, Massachusetts, which meant most of Turkey had cold, New England winters. I am not sure if any of us volunteers had thought of the ramifications of living in such conditions while in training, especially since our training was done in heavily forested Vermont. Later groups were brought to Turkey during training to acclimate them to the harsher conditions of Turkey's sub-zero winters and the hot, dry summers.

Peace Corps training did not prepare me for the reality of living in Turkey.

Clair, my female partner, and I were assigned to the village of Ismet Pasha. It was a progressive village because its inhabitants were actual descendants of Bulgarian Turks after the breakup of the Ottoman Empire in the 1920s. Many still had relatives there and were familiar with European culture and values, which

30

made it easier to communicate with them. But they retained their Muslim roots. The sexes did not mix outside of their families—except when the women worked in the fields during the harvest or served males and their guests at meals.

Ismet Pasha had neither electricity nor a paved road within ten kilometers. Its dirt road dead-ended in another, even poorer village. There were pine-forested mountains beyond it where wolves lurked. We were in the middle of the semi-arid (no more than 12 inches of annual rainfall) Anatolian Plateau that made up the heart of Turkey.

I had a backyard outhouse and a copious supply of both Lomotil and Kaopectate, the usual medications for dysentery. We were also given Tetracycline, an all-purpose antibiotic for more serious illnesses. I soon learned to boil all village water.

In theory we were to ferret out the so-called "wants and needs" of our community, a tenet of community development, and then search out those leaders who most wanted to find solutions to them. Building consensus in a community to solve a problem was a new concept to me, especially in a Turkish village that was only now evolving into the twentieth century. It didn't help that it took most of the first year to learn to speak enough of the Turkish language to make a meaningful difference.

Fortunately, the Turkish government intended to join the European Union. This meant Turkey had to adopt a daunting list of laws and regulations formulated by Europeans that were both social and economic: freedom of the press, the banning of torture (still practiced in some Turkish prisons), and abolition of the death penalty, among others.

Turkey was in a rush to modernize their society and saw a possible benefit in having young aid workers live and work in their countryside. This might help to bridge the enormous gap of knowledge between their fast-growing cities and a rural countryside where many still lived. Our rural community work might also slow the rush of villagers into the cities that were ill-prepared to receive them. Major ghettos grew around the larger cities, as is common in many developing countries. I was not even sure what could be done in a Turkish country village located halfway between Istanbul and Ankara. It was an almost treeless area on the Anatolian Plateau. The semi-arid climate meant little rain and snowfall, precluding a large variety of crops.

I would have to know a lot more about Turkish society as well as its agriculture to contribute to rural community development in any meaningful way.

The training lectures had given me a greater picture of Turkish history, which helped us to understand why we were in these villages. The urban cities of Turkey had followed Ataturk's lead in adopting western ways and some of its culture, whereas the villages were slower to adopt modern technologies. I saw the struggle women had in this ultra-male, Muslim culture, even though Turkey had become more western under Ataturk when he banned women wearing veils and men from wearing the fez, an Ottoman male's hat. Ataturk also pushed through Turkish women's right to vote even before the US and brought women into the first parliament created with formation of the Turkish Republic in 1925.

Turkey was the last vestige of the Ottoman Empire, and the Ottoman Dynasty had been its rulers since the Thirteenth Century. I enjoyed studying the many cultures and early civilizations that had occupied Turkey, such as Homer's Trojans and the Greeks of Alexander the Great that had first crossed into Asia Minor. Turkey's antique city of Ephesus was the capital of Rome's Asia Minor province, and Christians believed it held the tomb of St. John the Apostle. I even found remnants of Byzantine marble while roaming the remote hills and fields behind my village.

Who Was the Turkish Male?

Every healthy Turkish male was required to enlist in the Turkish armed forces. Turkish war veterans proudly displayed their medals, as well as wounds in photos I saw adorning walls in the Officer's Club in Eskisehir. There was a photo gallery of veteran amputees. They were usually seated in boxer shorts and undershirts to proudly display the stumps of limbs they had lost in battle.

Ten thousand American troops were stationed in Turkey facing Russia in the 1960s because of the NATO Alliance, and there was endless friction with Turks over their drinking and womanizing while living in segregated compounds.

Turkish veterans of the Korean War loved to tell me stories of their valor. The Turkish Brigade under NATO command acquitted itself heroically against North Korean and Chinese forces, which helped me to know about the Turkish men that I worked with.

Many Turkish, as well as American, soldiers were taken prisoner when the Chinese Army surprised General MacArthur by suddenly crossing the Yalu River border and driving back NATO forces to the 38th Parallel. The attempts at indoctrinating them with communist ideology in the prisoner-of-war camps were like those I had read in American studies of POWs in the Korean War—constant repetition of propaganda accompanied by hunger and sleep deprivation.

The studies concluded that Americans, though coming from a modern, individualistic society, were easier to convince to either sign a confession, or otherwise cooperate with their captors. But Turkish prisoners-of-war behaved differently, I was told. Whenever the Turkish soldiers' nominal commanding officer was removed from their POW group, they were able to maintain discipline because they had an age-old social hierarchy to fall back on. The next POW in that social order stepped up to lead them and maintain discipline.

I thought this might be bombast and did not want to politicize a POW story. I was not about to believe that American soldiers were any less brave than Turkish soldiers. But I listened because I wanted to learn as much about Turkish culture and history as possible.

Their tales were valuable in that they corroborated my observations in Ismet Pasha. Turks had more of a group-think mentality than Americans, so maybe such social bonding had made them less vulnerable to communist propaganda as North Korea's prisoners-of-war living under conditions not much harsher than those in their villages.

And I did corroborate some of these Turkish veterans' stories in later research on Korean POWs. A 1993 Texas Tech Master of Arts thesis summarized much of the research done by the US Army on the differences between US and Turkish POWs, as well as a citation from Eugene Kinkead's book *In Every War But One*.[1] The thesis read:

> "The Turks had an unusual record among the many United Nations prisoners: they maintained a strong cohesiveness and bonding throughout their captivity," said Kinkead of the Army study.
>
> Kinkead's book was based on a 5-year study of the effects of communist indoctrination on those held as prisoners of war in Korea, in which he concluded, "American POWs' performance in captivity suffered in comparison with the Turks' record. American prisoners of war who collaborated with the enemy acted strictly as individuals. Although there were notable exceptions, the Americans generally did not maintain unit and military discipline in their captivity."

[1] Kinkead, Eugene. *In Every War But One,* New York: W. W. Norton & Company, 1959. p. 158.

Community Development in Practice

Understanding Turkey's warrior ethos also helped me to understand how to make a difference in the village. Turkey was a hierarchical society in many ways outside of the military, with most major industries government owned at the time. But the county and provincial leaders (such as the sugar beet factory manager and agricultural ministry officials in Eskisehir) had little contact with the villagers, who were outside their sphere of influence.

The village Mukhtar (Mayor) was elected every five years in municipal elections independent of any political affiliation. So rural community development became an exercise in convincing independent-minded villagers of new practices that made sense to them.

I found therefore a tremendous knowledge gap between cities and rural countryside on what was possible to improve their lives, despite the tractors and harvester combines they already had obtained via the Marshall Plan. This was in part because there was little direct assistance from the governmental ministries. It was not until my second year that an agricultural agent visited the village to advise them that there were agricultural loans available to improve their livestock and crops.

Turkey did not have the much more decentralized U.S. state-run Agricultural Extension system of agents that directly advised farmers by visiting them on their farms. So, my villagers were mostly unaware of the latest research at the government-run research farms on what more productive crops, livestock, feeds, irrigation technology, education, vocational skills and handicrafts they could learn. These farmers knew how to conserve their meager resources but had no easily available knowledge of new ways to develop their land. Having no agricultural background myself, I looked for all the technical help I could get to make any kind of difference in Ismet Pasha.

Fortunately, I had an uncle from Texas who was a cattle rancher that I could rely on for advice in what might be possible. He sent me catalogues of modern farming equipment, which gave the village farmers some understanding of modern farming techniques. My uncle's part of Texas had similar climate and soil conditions, which meant some of his crop recommendations could improve Ismet Pasha's crops as well, which impressed the villagers.

In sharing lives with these villagers, I came to appreciate what they could do with what they had. In a semi-arid climate without irrigation water, the villagers practiced what were called dry farming techniques, which entailed planting their wheat, oats, and barley in the spring once the ground thawed. This meant winter was a fallow time, so I spent the short days and long, cold winter nights learning enough Turkish to understand what they were asking for and communicating my ideas on how to get them done.

Since we had arrived in November, there was plenty of time to figure out just what kind of projects were possible with farmers that already had everything they needed to grow dry farming crops. There were truck drivers, a blacksmith to repair the plows, and a mechanic to keep at least half a dozen tractors

37

running: machinery that the villagers had obtained via the Marshall Plan in the late 1940s and early 1950s.

Our program was supervised by the CARE organization which gave us some status. CARE was well known in Turkey because it provided a school lunch program for Turkish school children, and I could see why CARE was so highly regarded. It was one of the largest American organizations outside of the Red Cross and UNESCO that had any experience in foreign aid and assistance at the grass roots level—which meant living outside of the cities where most American aid workers, including most Peace Corps Volunteers, lived and worked.

CARE had been distributing food, clothing and tools donated by Americans to Turkey since the 1950s. I even remember my parents putting together CARE packages to feed children still suffering during and after World War II. But American volunteers were now the "aid packages" CARE distributed, instead of clothing and tools.

Community development principles were just now coming to the fore in foreign aid circles, and Washington as well as academia wanted to know if they could work in developing countries at the so-called grass roots level of age-old agrarian societies, and so we became the Guinea pigs for this experiment, often visited by social scientists and anthropologists who wanted to know how we were succeeding.

Our Work in Ismet Pasha

I was assigned to Ismet Pasha, the home village of the oldest son of the wealthiest landowner Suleyman Alkan. Suleyman was the Provincial Director of their Vocational Education programs. These vocational courses traveled from village to village with instructors, and two were in Ismet Pasha that first year—a carpentry and woodworking course for the men and machine sewing, canning (there was no electricity, hence refrigeration), and rug weaving instruction for the women.

Rug weaving was an art that had died out in many parts of Turkey. The Kilim rug was their most common rug, woven mostly from rags, yet just a few old women still practiced the craft.

Clair, my female volunteer counterpart, assisted in the elementary school and taught English to those who might go on to a Middle or High School in the provincial capital of Eskisehir after they completed the required minimum eighth grade education.

Turkish women received a basic elementary education to the eighth grade but little else, unless they were from a wealthy family. They were usually married and bearing children by 14 years of age, which yielded large families. A woman was considered old when she turned forty, and her children full-grown.

Clair's job was more difficult than mine. There was not one female CARE or Peace Corps staff member to support the female volunteers in Turkey during that time. Clair left in the second year, partially because of this lack of support. She had fallen in love with a volunteer in another village. Because marriage or any kind of cohabitation of single couples was forbidden during our Peace Corps service, they opted to end their service and return to the U.S. to marry. The Peace Corps lost two very caring volunteers who could have contributed so much more working together and completing their service, but the stricture on singles marrying while in service was short-sighted. It was incredible that we—supposed models of modernity—were neglectful in fully utilizing the potential of our own female counterparts.

Mustafa Kemal Ataturk had passed laws that gave women the right to vote at the establishment of the Turkish Republic and women were elected to be members of the Turkish Republic's first parliament. But village women still tended to shroud their faces when around strange males. A Vocational Education instructor and visiting midwife were the only Turkish women in the villages to wear conventional western clothing that I ever saw.

I initially fit into the woodworking and metal working classes since I had worked as a carpenter. I designed, and we built, the first washing machine for the women. It used a plunger to agitate the water and was quite the occasion when first demonstrated. Until then the village women could only wash clothes in a tub, or at the village fountain, pounding clothing on the rocks.

It was obvious that Ismet Pasha needed irrigation water if the villagers wanted to grow more than wheat, oats, and barley. Their wells were hand-dug and no more than 40 feet deep before hitting hard bedrock. A single, spring-fed fountain in the village center supplied their households and livestock with drinking water.

Curiously, villages closer to Eskisehir, the provincial capital and largest city, had irrigation water and grew sugar beets which were processed in Eskisehir's large sugar beet factory. Irrigation water was therefore probably accessible near Ismet Pasha if the villagers had the tools to find it.

The pine-forested mountains behind the village had to be part of a watershed that held underground water. A visit to the government Agricultural Ministry that held the records of other irrigation wells had maps and charts showing the area as a watershed for the Sakarya River, one of Turkey's major rivers that flowed north into the Black Sea. A tributary flowed approximately 10 kilometers away. I thought there had to be water flowing in aquifers beneath Ismet Pasha.

It took a year to research the possibilities of finding such a water source and convince the villagers it was a good idea. They tried drilling with a posthole auger, as my dad and I had done at home, but the auger couldn't get through the underlying hard rock layer that had prevented their hand dug wells from going any deeper. I would have to convince the villagers to pay for expensive well-drilling equipment that could drill through hard rock. The rig was only available from the large sugar beet factory in Eskisehir.

I made a bet with the Factory Manager. He was so confident they could find water with their expensive deep-well rig that he agreed to charge the villagers just half of the normal price per foot if no water was found. The villagers considered this to be a fair negotiation. Two wells were dug before they found good water. It was under such pressure beneath the rock layers that it shot to the surface when the drill punched through the rock. There was then a huge celebration as the farmers and their families came out to see with their own eyes what they thought was impossible. That one well supplied enough water to irrigate at least 160 hectares of vegetables and other crops, which was a tremendous flow.

I found that the villagers were eager to learn when they had access to new methods. Nothing seemed to be too outrageous to try in our Rural Community Development group in those days. One volunteer in the lusher western coastal area was able to export an abundance of snails from their village to France, with its love of escargot.

Chapter Four

The Second Year Is Most Difficult

A whole year passed before I began to see any results from my work in Ismet Pasha. There was a modern Agricultural Experimental Farm in the nearest market town where I could obtain the latest seeds and farming methods, though most villagers were reluctant to visit the experimental farms, which were few and far between. Their reluctance was one reason there was such an immense knowledge gap between city and country, which made my work more meaningful. A Turkish agricultural advisor from their Agricultural Ministry didn't visit Ismet Pasha until the second year to advise and offer them agricultural loans.

Ismet Pasha was located where there were frequent blizzards in winter and occasional flash floods in the spring and summer. It was said a lightning strike during a violent thunderstorm once killed the family patriarch while sitting at the head of the table during dinner, and a woman drowned in her garden during a flash flood.

The inclement weather meant I spent a lot of time in the village coffee houses trying to convince more farmers to attempt a new crop, or better livestock, or new farming technique, as

43

well as drill more wells. I convinced several to visit an Israeli chicken breeder to see what was possible. We struck a deal with the breeder: he agreed to buy back the grown broilers at market prices if they were delivered in good health.

During the nights that blizzards howled outside, the women and children had to sleep beside a coal-fed breeder stove to keep the new chicks at just the right temperature. I had constructed such a coal stove with a metal umbrella under which the chicks huddled to keep warm. Raising chicks in midwinter was not something the villagers had imagined could be done.

I was careful to divide my time between the two coffee houses (really a misnomer, since tea, not coffee, was served, as coffee was imported and expensive). The coffee houses were frequented only by men, where they clustered around tables drinking endless rounds of tea and playing backgammon while discussing the business of the day. It was really the result of those long winter discussions that I was able to enlist the younger members to try out new ideas.

Learning the Turkish Village Culture

Most Turks still lived in the rural villages at that time, and little research existed on village social structures. Several social anthropologists had asked that we village volunteers keep detailed diaries they might access for their research. Some of them did visit us during our stay and published papers on rural Turkish life and culture before it disappeared with Turkey's modernization push.

MIT Professor Richard Robinson, a historian and social anthropologist, had studied Turkish village life and was interested enough in our work to visit and document what we were doing. His studies, such as *The First Turkish Republic,* were classics in the field and required reading for those who wanted to know how Turkey became a western-style republic.[1]

But the work wore me down in the second year, as it did for many of the volunteers in our group. With Clair gone that second year, I had no other volunteers nearby I could talk to. I had no access to a telephone. There was a single line in the Mukhtar's office, but who could I call? I don't remember that volunteers in the cities—who were mostly teachers and health care workers—had much access to phones, either.

I could hop onto the daily bus that came by in the morning and travel either to the nearest market town (about one hour's drive) or to Eskisehir to see the sights and visit other volunteers. A Peace Corps Volunteer group was teaching English as a Second Language in the Eskisehir high schools. I could always stay with them in their modern apartments when I tired of village life.

The villagers understood how lonely I felt in the second year without Clair to talk to. I had many invites to dine with a family. The food was relatively plentiful in Ismet Pasha, and some of the healthiest in the world. Their own yogurt came from sheep or goat milk. Villages closer to the Mediterranean or Aegean Seas had much richer yogurt made from water buffalo milk with a fifteen percent butter fat content that was as rich as sour cream.

---

[1] Robinson, Richard. *The First Turkish Republic: A Case Study in National Development* (Cambridge, Mass.: 1963)

45

There were the goat, sheep, and cow cheeses, compotes made from local sundried fruits; grains for pilaf or couscous, and a soup of hot milk containing vermicelli sprinkled with cayenne pepper that usually started off the meal.

Stone-ground bread from the village's own flour mill was a complete meal in itself. A large round, one-kilo loaf came steaming from the oven at mealtime. It is the sacred food of the Koran (a sheaf of wheat tempted Eve instead of the apple), so its crumbs and leftovers were never wasted but sprinkled in the fields or given to livestock.

There were several varieties of beans, a large, hot chili pepper that was cooked in milk, and lots of okra and eggplant. Beef was not plentiful, and the steaks were extremely small (called filets), but fresh lamb and goat meat was usually available and eaten soon after slaughter, since there was no electricity for refrigeration. Meat was usually served on a steaming platter of rice pilaf or roasted on a spit as a kebab.

All this was placed on a very short-legged, circular table rolled out at mealtime, and around which the men sat cross-legged. The family's women served us but otherwise ate separately, at least when a strange male was present.

Each person was given a large spoon and either tore off or cut their portion of the loaf of bread. The tablecloth draped over our laps served as a napkin, and we always ate from a common bowl or platter. Alcohol was almost never served at meals in the villages, as the Koran was most explicit about its evils. But we did drink Turkish Raki, a licorice-flavored drink, when in the fields during the harvest. It was called "lion's milk" because it turned white when diluted with water.

The food was delicious, and every stranger or acquaintance was treated as an honored guest, such is a mainstay of the Islamic code of conduct. Time and again I saw that these farmers shared what they had freely with a heartfelt generosity that particularly helped me through the second year.

The villagers also looked out for our health, I discovered that first winter. I contracted the Asian flu at the beginning of both winters, also called the Grippe in Europe and Asia, a particularly virulent flu strain. The first time was terrifying. After a night of feverish hallucinations, I was found sweat-soaked by someone, too weak to even lift my arms. I do not remember who discovered me in that helpless state, but I was immediately bundled into a blanket and thrown in the back of a trailer towed by a tractor through foot-deep snow. I was taken directly to a Turkish doctor who operated a government clinic in the nearest town ten kilometers distant.

Peace Corps staff castigated me when they learned of my Turkish care because, for some reason, Peace Corps Volunteers were told not to use Turkish doctors. The U.S. Air Force had an American hospital in Eskisehir, one hour's drive, that was on a NATO air base, but I wanted to live as Turkish villagers lived. I found that stricture absurd. After all, if we volunteers could not trust and be treated by Turks suffering similar ailments, how were we to relate to them, much less have them trust us?

It turned out the wife of the doctor was also the Mayor of the town which had the health clinic I visited. It was a bonus, as visiting this Turkish doctor rather than running to the nearest American doctor gave me more standing in the community. It also illustrated the difference in station between educated Turkish women and village women.

The Turkish doctor gave me a penicillin shot for the Grippe. It seemed to be their cure-all for everything, including dog bites. He told me he had recently treated a serious dog bite from one of the ferocious Anatolian sheep dogs by placing penicillin powder on the wound. I remember from training that it would require a painful series of rabies shots if we were ever bitten by a dog in Turkey.

I was in fact attacked by such a sheep dog that year. I liked to take long walks in good weather to explore the back country and had been cautioned to be careful in my wanderings and listen for sheep bells since the herds were usually guarded by a Turkish sheep dog. They were Anatolian Mastiffs, a well-recognized breed that wore one-inch spike collars to protect them from wolf attacks in the fields.

If I heard the tinkling of sheep bells, I was told to only approach a herd on the shepherd's side, since these mastiffs were known for their aggressive behavior protecting the herds from the marauding wolves still prevalent in Turkey.

On one such day I was more engrossed in the spring scenery and wasn't listening for sheep bells when I came over a hill where a small herd of sheep grazed just below me. I saw that the shepherd was located on the other side of the herd and the sheep dog on my side. The dog immediately charged me, and all I could do in those few seconds was fall to the ground and cover my head.

I was saved from any mauling by the shepherd, who had a very accurate throwing arm. He launched his shepherd's long staff at his sheepdog while running towards me. It was a javelin throw that miraculously knocked the mastiff aside in midair just as it leaped for me.

Learning the Turkish Culture

Turkey was a completely foreign world, one that I had known nothing about when I volunteered. It was a journey of discovery into a continent that was completely opposite to western ways and thought. Yet it was the most western-oriented Asian country because it bridged Europe and Asia geographically.

I most vividly remember the contrast when crossing back from Greece, where I would spend time during vacations. This small dose of European culture lifted my spirits immensely.

I enjoyed the Greeks on the nearby island of Lesbos that I visited, a short boat ride from the Turkish coast. They were a happy people with their friendly smiles and lilting music. Returning to Turkey I would be met by a crowd of somber and guarded faces, a sea of identical blank expressions of the Turkish men that never seemed to vary.

There was little nightlife outside of Ankara and Istanbul for volunteers living in the countryside, which meant we sought other volunteers for companionship when not in the villages.

49

The taboo on sex by single male volunteers with American or Turkish women was strenuously emphasized—at least while we were working in the villages. We were told we would be living in a fishbowl, where every Turkish woman was a virgin until she married, and Turkish men had very little interaction with them, unless related.

Every major industry in Turkey was government-owned at the time. Turkey had a Soviet-style five-year economic plan that regulated everything from cigarettes, heavy industry, and alcohol to coal mines, and the world's "oldest female profession".

Few of the males that I knew tried out the government-licensed brothels for sex, even though the Peace Corps made sure male volunteers had been provided with a large package of condoms (at least a dozen packets, if I remember), in case we were in danger of contracting a sexually transmitted disease. It was something besides rabies and tapeworms that we should worry about.

One had the choice of Class A through C brothels, depending on affordability (and frequency of medical inspections of the prostitutes by government doctors). A walk-through of Ankara's compound was like stepping into a Fellini movie with its carnival-like atmosphere. (Fellini movies such as La Dolce Vita were popular in those days.) The brothels were called compounds because they were usually surrounded by high walls. One entered through a gate or metal door guarded by a local policeman, the only sign of state ownership. Inside, very narrow streets were lined by small, gaudily decorated cottages that belonged to each prostitute, who stood displaying her wares in a scanty harem outfit if she was waiting for customers.

I preferred different entertainments. One major event that last winter was Ramadan, the Muslim Lent. Ramadan was a month of fasting and prayer from sunrise to sunset; no food or drink allowed during the time they were to remember the sufferings of Mohammed, their desert prophet. Absolutely nothing was to pass their lips, I was told, except water, unless they were on a travel that precluded such fasting. But come sunset, the nightlong celebrations of food and festivities began. Their world was turned topsy-turvy, and they loved it.

I remember riding on a bus during one Ramadan sunset. The hands of the passenger next to me shook slightly as he prepared for his first tobacco of the day. He had placed a large pinch of snuff (powdered tobacco) on the back of his hand, carefully arranging it between thumb and forefinger.

Others were noisily opening their various meal packages. The moment the bus radio finished blaring the Muezzin's evening prayer my companion inhaled his snuff in one huge snort and began coughing and sneezing uncontrollably. This roused a few snickers from those seated nearest to us as they ate their prepared meals.

Ismet Pasha's villagers celebrated in their own ways. Each family that could afford it would host an evening meal where some of their wonderful desserts were prepared. We were served Halvah, a cake-like substance made of flour and sugar, or Borek, a delicious thin-shelled meat or cheese-filled pastry common

51

in the Mediterranean, or Pishmane, a nutritious cotton candy. Pishmane was prepared by first pouring hot, caramelized sugar syrup into clean snow, where it congealed. It was then pulled into thin strands in the cold air, before being stirred into a mix of flour and pistachios. It was magically transformed into a cloud of cotton candy before our eyes.

After the evening meal came the games. One favorite was "Button, button, who has the button," with much skillful sleight of hand, so that my palm would burn from being slapped with a ruler when not guessing which fist held the button. It was a painful penalty.

It was becoming obvious that I wasn't tolerating village life well by the end of my second year. Though I involved myself as much as possible in village activities, I began to make longer trips to visit other volunteers to know what they were seeing and doing.

I was even anxious when riding the buses for fear of being in an accident, becoming a nervous wreck who smoked a pack-a-day of their four-cent packs of "Soldier" cigarettes. The brand name was the Turkish word for soldier, and I never knew if it was created to provide the poorly paid Turkish soldier with something he could afford.

The tediousness of becoming a single volunteer was spelled by 45 days of paid vacation leave allowed by the Peace Corps during the two years of service, and semi-annual conferences brought everyone together for progress reports.

Our own volunteer liaisons were made during holidays and our vacations. We village volunteers were considered well paid at 60 dollars per month, the equivalent of a Turkish teacher's salary. To put that in perspective, we could have a good restaurant meal for one dollar, and a haircut for 25 cents. In addition, we were allowed $7.50 per day of vacation allowance. I had money to travel on, as my rent for a small, one room adobe cottage was just $3 per month that second year.

A female volunteer and I overstayed our vacation time on the island of Rhodes during the winter school break because of a severe Mediterranean storm that capsized a tourist boat with the loss of 40 lives. It also meant she was late in returning to her teaching classes.

I was reprimanded for assisting in her delinquency through no fault of her own, and our Peace Corps country director at the time withdrew his offer to put me on training staff after completion of my two years. My loneliness had cost me the possibility of remaining in Turkey for a third year.

Not spending another year in Turkey was probably a good thing, as I was feeling more sad than happy as my two years of service came to an end. As difficult as it was to live in and absorb so much of a foreign culture, it was just as difficult to leave such an intensely emotional experience.

We of Turkey V, the first volunteer rural community development group to serve in any Muslim country, were finally discharged in June of 1966, and it could not have been a day later for me.

Had I made a difference, and what did the villagers end up thinking of me? There were so many highs and lows—the companionship with other volunteers that broke the tedium of village life, the travel, visits to ancient, storied civilizations, and being part of such an ancient way of life that was barely changed by a few tractors and combines to speed up the planting and harvest.

Turkey in Later Years

As the Vietnam War dragged on, Americans and the American way did not look so peaceful to the rest of the world. This was one reason Peace Corps left Turkey after 10 years during which some 1600 hundred volunteers had served.

Opposition to the Vietnam War had grown in many European countries, and educated Turkish students were no exception. There were also serious gaffes by American officials, such as appointing former CIA employee Robert Comer to be the next U.S. Ambassador to Turkey. He had overseen the South Vietnamese village pacification plan, and his appointment as Ambassador to Turkey so enraged students that they overturned and burned his car during one of the many anti-war protests.

His predecessor, our own Peace Corps director, had earlier killed an elderly woman dressed in black, while driving in Ankara one dark and rainy night. Because he had diplomatic immunity, he was spirited out of Turkey to avoid being charged with manslaughter.

That was not well-received by the students, either. Turkey and the Peace Corps administration agreed it was time to phase out the Peace Corps program that had lasted from 1961 to 1971.

My last year had been a very lonely, but productive, year, and I had no illusions that most villagers in this part of Anatolia with its semi-arid and mostly treeless environment would stay in their villages much longer. Their industrial revolution was now in full swing.

I hoped our presence there as volunteers had helped them consider us as their friends rather than obnoxious foreigners. I also hoped they saw us presenting a better, more peaceful side of American foreign policy that was more in line with the truthful face of the America I believed in.

I believe the Peace Corps Volunteers serving in Turkey did make a difference. We encouraged many of our villagers to work to develop their own land, instead of moving to the cities. These villagers were usually the most prosperous landowners that could exploit more modern farming techniques.

There was also talk of the Turks forming their own domestic volunteer corps that had a Turkish precedent. Educated Turkish males could choose to teach in a village school instead of wearing a military uniform because Turkey had universal male military conscription. But I never knew if that happened, in part because Turkey was changing so fast.

A Return to Turkey

Even today Turkey's rural population has continued to grow, though the percentage of the total population living in villages has declined because of rural-to-urban migration.

In 1970 about 67 percent of the population lived in villages. In 1980 the rural population had declined to 54 percent. Less than 21 percent of Turkey's population still lived in villages in 2020, according to the World Bank.

This is why I was so startled on a return trip to Turkey. More than 30 years had passed since I left in 1966 and I wanted to know what remained of my work in Ismet Pasha. I had organized a tour group that landed at Istanbul's Ataturk Airport during a national holiday. It was a shock to see the streets lined with many women covered from head to foot in traditional clothing as we were driven to our hotel. They had to be from the villages to dress so conservatively. It was evidence of the mass migration to cities and how much Istanbul, Turkey's most European and cosmopolitan city, had changed.

I made a point of visiting Ismet Pasha during the tour, but it seemed a shell of its former self on my return. The mill that produced their flour was gone, a sign of the decline of village life. It meant the villagers no longer baked their own stone ground wheat bread into giant kilo loaves steaming just out of the oven that I had enjoyed so much when invited to dine with them.

The ethnic Turks who still lived in Ismet Pasha, including the son of the Mukhtar I had worked with during my two years, were doing well. Irrigation water was now plentiful from a fully developed irrigation system that watered a large sugar beet crop via elevated concrete canals that funneled water into the fields.

But the village was also full of Kurds transplanted from their homeland in eastern Turkey. They were the victims of the ongoing war with Kurdish militants belonging to the PKK, their most radical political party that wanted an independent country of their own.

The war had dragged on for years and did not look like it would come to any resolution soon, since millions of Kurds still lived in Turkey and were forbidden to teach their language in the schools.

The ethnic Turks to whom I spoke looked down on the Kurds as bad farmers, transplants that really did not fit in. The Kurds were thought of as a semi-nomadic herding culture, since many of them lived in the mountains of Syria, Iran, and Turkey. But maybe it was also because all the good land around Ismet Pasha had been developed by the largest families who were able to take advantage of the new irrigation water I first brought to the village?

Ismet Pasha and most of the remote rural villages now have electricity and paved roads that give them greater access to markets for their produce in all seasons, so their economic future looks bright.

But will Turkey ever become a sectarian democracy ruled by civil law rather than religious law? Or will they be saddled with their current devoutly religious President, Recep Tayyip Erdoğan, an aspiring President-for-life, intent on imposing a more religious theocracy rather than continuing their sputtering attempts to join the European Union?

I also saw that the community development precepts I learned in Peace Corps training worked in a Turkish village, because they were much like us, a practical people who believed success in the secular world was as important as the world promised by Islam. Who knows what future might be possible for such a hardworking people?

I felt good about what I had come to do, and it was now time to move on to other challenges.

Chapter Five

Berkeley's Last Riot

I lived in Germany for one year after leaving Turkey because I was still eligible for the draft. I had heard stories of Peace Corps Volunteers being drafted on their return to the U.S. if they were under the age of 26, and I hadn't passed that age threshold yet. It was 1967 and the Vietnam War was still raging.

I married and earned a Masters Degree in Film/Broadcasting from Boston University after returning to America, but another four years passed before I returned to a changed Berkeley.

It was now 1972, and President Nixon was about to be reelected. Even though he promised to end the Vietnam War, he had ordered the bombing of Hanoi since June 1972. His Secretary of State Henry Kissinger thought bombing North Vietnam's capital and neighboring Laos might obtain a more favorable armistice deal for the U.S. and South Vietnam, but the North Vietnamese were refusing to negotiate until the bombs stopped falling.

American B-52s bombed Hanoi and its surroundings several times; the worst happened with an almost continuous onslaught from December 18 to December 29, except for an 18-hour pause at Christmas.

Bach Mai, one of Hanoi's major hospitals, had been hit with what was essentially carpet bombing that leveled large sections of the densely populated city. Western journalists were covering it, and several anti-war groups visited Hanoi that autumn to publicize the horrendous damage that was killing doctors and nurses as well as ordinary citizens.

That was when I found out the anti-war crowd in Berkeley was still very much alive. Its residents were so outraged over the bombings that a proposal was put to Warren Widener's Berkeley City Council to donate $1,000 to Hanoi's Bach Mai Hospital that had been badly damaged in earlier bombings.

And the city council meeting was to be held in the Berkeley Community Theater that held 3,491 spectators.

I had no idea I would be witnessing what I believe was Berkeley's last full scale, anti-war rally. It felt as if I had emerged from a time capsule into a much more chaotic America still caught up in Vietnam. The quiet, middle class, mostly white Berkeley suburb I had left in 1966 when I joined the Peace Corps was gone. The new Berkeley was more racially mixed and had just elected Warren Widener as its first Black mayor, reflecting the changed population mix.

I saw a Berkeley that exuded a sense of despair and desperation, almost the opposite of the Berkeley I remembered.

The first indication that something more than an ordinary council meeting was anticipated was the presence of flatbed trucks loaded with plywood panels prowling Berkeley's Telegraph Avenue. Berkeley's storekeepers were boarding up their windows and doors. The sounds of pounding hammers and screeching saws reverberated everywhere. I remember it was a normal shopping day, which turned out to be the calm before a storm.

I attended because I was excited to see what might happen after witnessing Boston's 1970 Earth Day riot that began as an anti-war rally on the Boston Commons while I was still a student at Boston University. There was serious looting and storefront fires with crowd estimates of up to 3,000, that rioted and burned several buildings when they reached Harvard Square, according to the *Harvard Crimson*. A nighttime curfew was established when the rioting and looting continued past midnight.

It was a shock to me because I had no idea a peaceful anti-war rally could turn violent so quickly until that Earth Day riot. So I wasn't surprised at what happened on my return to Berkeley.

The vote over the proposed donation was held on the stage of a packed Berkely Community Theater. Berkeley's city council members seemed oblivious to the possible consequences. The council was deadlocked, with the deciding vote a "no" vote cast by the newest member, Mayor Widener's replacement on the council, defeating the proposal.

The enraged audience poured out of the theater, set on destroying what they could in a city they now considered corrupt for not providing even token support to the Vietnamese people who had suffered for so long.

Police had been stationed on the City Hall roof just blocks away, as the crowd began streaming out of the auditorium that evening. A bonfire was already burning on the City Hall steps in a possible attempt to burn it down. The Police opened fire with rubber bullets at those closest to it. The crowd panicked and surged forward. I followed, wanting to see what would happen next.

Shattuck Avenue was further away, the main east-west shopping artery in Berkeley where the BART subway from San Francisco surfaced. The avenue became the natural target of the angry crowd with its large, gleaming plate glass auto showroom windows. They hadn't been boarded up. Perhaps the Shattuck merchants weren't accustomed to teargassed protests and marches.

Berkeley was once again a war zone. Shattered plate glass littered the streets of Shattuck Avenue and its intersection with University Avenue after the crowd melted away into the morning mist.

The rest of that night is a hazy memory from a long time ago. The Berkeley of the last riot on that May day was a different city from the one I had known. The anger I saw in the attempt to burn down City Hall and to destroy the major shopping district was a last desperate act.

This was 1972, and Governor Ronald Reagan had used California's National Guard to literally beat down anti-war protests since he became Governor in 1966. The show of force did little to tamp down the anti-war sentiment. Two days later, Berkeley's streets were as crowded and chaotic as ever, its people used to a war that had really been fought for the hearts and minds of Americans.

Berkeley's "natives" still wore tie dye clothes (or no clothes), long hair, sandals or bare feet along Telegraph Ave, the pulsing artery that connected California's Golden Bears with the real world. It was what I had left in 1964; it was still a place that believed in peace and freedom, but now it seemed exhausted from the battles for peace and freedom that I thought had been won.

So much of the U.S. had fragmented into competing communities of the rich and poor on my return, with many gated communities adjacent to gutted homes. The Vietnam War wasn't winding down, as Nixon promised, but even so, Berkeley had changed. Governor Ronald Reagan and the UC Regents began charging tuition at the state universities. That meant only more affluent students could afford to attend, which was no doubt the intention of the conservative Regents. Because students had to worry about tuition and student loan debts, they were more careful about voicing their views.

I wrote a poem about the impact of Berkeley's last major anti-war riot. It recalled many memories of my student days and reignited my passion for service that I would carry forward in coming decades. Returning to Berkeley brought back memories of my enthusiasm that anything was possible if I believed it was a worthy cause.

Kennedy's presidency had been a unifying event that motivated me and others to serve. It was the beginning of what he called the New Frontier of possibilities. It was the same spirit that had brought on the civil rights movement resulting in President Johnson's Voting Rights Act and the War on Poverty.

Berkeley's Last Riot

Somehow Berkeley knew,

City of Cal's Golden Bears,

That had weathered countless Free Speech protests,

Anti-war marches,

And sit-ins.

The City of People's Park knew,

When those storefronts were boarded up,

Cody's Books all-glass façade,

When the masked police appeared

With tear-gas canisters.

They knew

Something would happen,

When Berkeley's Warren Widener

Decided to stage a public vote,

Its First Black Mayor.

The vote

In Berkeley's Community Theatre,

To give North Vietnam 1,000 dollars

For its Bach Mai Hospital,

Bombed by Nixon's B-52s.

Berkeley knew something would

Happen when its citizens perched

Above the huge stage

Not one of the 3,491 seats empty,

To watch the drama unfold.

Berkeley's City Council vote to give aid,

Was put on display

For all to see,

That Hanoi's citizens,

Had been bombed by Nixon's B-52s.

It was living Theatre,

That evening drama in its finest hour,

Acted by the people,

For the people,

Of Vietnam.

Berkeley knew what would happen,

When the no vote came,

A tiebreaker cast by its newest member.

What was she thinking,

With 28 pharmacists, nurses and doctors'

Lives lost that Christmas at Bach Mai hospital

From Nixon's B-52s?

So no it was to Hanoi's hospital,

And no it was to Berkeley's full house,

That stormed out that night

To destroy the city that was no longer,

For the people anymore.

First burn down City Hall was the cry,

Just a block away,

Burn it down,

But rubber bullets from its roof

Drove them away.

Away from the burning steps,

To Shattuck Ave,

With its Cadillac showrooms,

And University Avenue,

Busting every plate glass window.

Berkeley was their city no longer in 1972.

The people had lost

To Nixon's B-52s,

And history,

In Berkeley's last riot.

I soon found a job teaching film at San Francisco City College. It gave me a brief respite from social activism, but not for long. A neighbor I had grown up with who happened to work in the General Services Administration called to ask if I was interested in a job with the US Environmental Protection Agency. Would I like to use my filmmaking skills in protecting the environment?

Chapter Six

The Great Clean Air Debate:

Early Years of US Environmental

Protection Agency

I joined the United States Environmental Protection Agency (USEPA) in 1972, two years after the Clean Air Act was passed. I had a graduate degree in film and had been teaching courses at San Francisco City College as well as working as a news cameraman for a Sacramento TV station. For the EPA I would make films and photograph whatever promoted cleaner air and water.

Paul DeFalco, the Western Regional Administrator, had been looking for someone to record and publicize the EPA in action. In those early days of the environmental movement, the EPA offices were in a small building at the foot of Nob Hill. I was hired as a jack-of-all trades to produce slide shows, photographic exhibits, and films to educate the public on the new Clean Air Act and Clean Water regulations.

To say those early years with the EPA's Ninth District was an exciting time is an understatement. I could travel anywhere in California, or Nevada, or Arizona in the Western District if I needed to photograph a polluting oil tanker, or refinery, that might be leaking effluent into San Francisco Bay, the Pacific Ocean, or any other body of water in those states.

This seemed to be a worthy cause for a former Peace Corps Volunteer who had served in Turkey. The USEPA was just the ticket. I was always finding opportunities to photograph distant sites, as well as air documentaries and public service ads on television and other media. I could hitch rides on Coast Guard helicopters, and even on their seaplane when they made patrols over water.

Environmental Protection Could be Hazardous

At the time, I remember thinking environmental protection should not mean crawling down the partially opened rear stairs of a Boeing 727 passenger jet into a muddy field at San Francisco International Airport.

I had boarded a regularly scheduled Sunday afternoon flight to Los Angeles where I was producing a one-half hour public service television show for the USEPA on the dangers of toxic substances in anything we might eat or drink.

I sat next to a World War II pilot on that cloudy, rainy day in a United Airlines 727. Wisps of clouds raced by as we ascended. I hated the 727 with its three engines in the rear of the plane. It took off and landed like a wounded duck, as far as I was concerned, yet the airlines used it for the shorter flights. It always seemed to land with a deep thud that made me close my eyes on the approach, wondering if it had landed safely, and it seemed to lift off at the very last moment from the end of the runway.

As we climbed, I noticed a vapor streaming from the wing tips. I pointed it out to the former pilot I had just met. He said not to worry too much: they were probably jettisoning some excess fuel.

"But why?" I asked. "Why would they be jettisoning fuel after the takeoff?" It wasn't long before we knew the answer. The pilot's voice came over the intercom: "We don't want you to be alarmed, but we have to return to the airport."

I looked at my seat partner who seemed calm. He had been regaling me with stories of his fighter pilot days in World War II in the Pacific. "I don't know what it could be," he said. "Probably some malfunction in the navigation system, or some of the dials aren't giving accurate signals."

That was when the airline pilot told us what was actually happening. "We are returning because a warning light is telling us something is overheating in the cargo bay," he said over the intercom. "It may be nothing, a light malfunctioning, but we would like you to grab your ankles as we approach landing, just in case."

That was possible when flying in the 1970s. Seats were farther apart. In fact, airlines competed to offer more leg room rather than less in those days.

Though my heart beat a little faster, I didn't think anything could really be wrong. But my partner and I grabbed our ankles as we approached, just in case. The plane had been circling while continuing to jettison fuel.

We heard the landing gear lock and the jet engines reverse thrust to slow down the plane as we landed, so I thought the flight was over. Suddenly there was a much louder THUNK, then the plane tilted crazily and began to slowly rotate. Those of us grabbing our ankles could see nothing, but I had the sickening feeling that I was going to die.

The THUNK was followed by a screeching of metal, but I had no idea how long that lasted before the silence. It was a silence that I honestly thought meant the end—I think we all felt that way—even though my mind was racing. Was it even possible this was what the afterlife must be? A limbo of sorts with nothing to see or hear? It was as if, at that moment, I had left my body, and whatever had become of me was hovering overhead.

But then I heard screaming, and a group of uniformed pilots suddenly appeared out of nowhere. It was only later that I realized they were off-duty pilots hitching rides home on the weekend. At this moment they happened to be in the right place at the right time. At least six of them rousted passengers out of their seats.

Most of us were in shock. They had to literally grab some of the passengers and throw them down the inflated chutes that had opened before it dawned on the rest of us that we needed to get the hell out of there.

Being near the tail of this 727, my partner and I had only one escape route. There was an exit staircase that opened under the tail, but it was only partially open. We crawled our way down those steps and found that the tail was sitting in the mud. When we stood up to look around in a slight drizzle, hands and knees covered in the mud, we saw we were in a wet field beside one of the runways. The nose of the plane was buried in a small, corrugated metal shack that must have stopped its slide.

My partner said immediately, "It has to be one of the landing gear."

"What landing gear?" I asked. I looked up and down the runway we were beside and saw no landing gear. My partner had taken out a miniature Minolta camera and began clicking away in all directions as people continued to crawl or slide out of the plane. Some lay on the ground moaning, as sirens from approaching rescue vehicles screamed louder.

The pilots and crew members herded us away from the fuselage. I saw no smoke, and so thank God, maybe no fire. They were also shouting, "No pictures, please, no pictures, please," which my partner, of course, ignored. When I looked down the runway that crossed ours, I saw a small object lying in the middle of it. It was our landing gear: four wheels still locked to the strut that anchored it to the wing.

The right-side wing was buried in the ground, and we now could see what had happened. Its landing gear, with all four wheels, had broken off the wing and was laying with its strut assembly barely visible in the distance. We must have skidded for more than a mile before coming to a stop in this muddy field.

The ex-fighter pilot told me that he had once crash landed on a beach and broken his back in the Philippines during World War II. It underscored how lucky we were this time. The United pilot must have landed too soon with too much fuel in the tanks. I had flown enough to know planes usually take off with more fuel than is safe to carry when landing, in case they were stuck in a holding pattern before descending to the tarmac. The extra weight may have caused the wounded duck to hit the runway harder than was safe. But the pilot's skill probably saved us by keeping the plane's nose up, said my seat mate, despite the impact that could have flipped us end-over-end.

So I cancelled the television show that weekend, even though United Airlines offered to put me on the next plane to Los Angeles—once the runways were cleared.

There was no map of what we should or could do in those early days. But making the public aware of what was happening to our air and water was a priority. Administrator DeFalco wanted the public to know why we were here and what needed to be done to protect the environment.

It was the dawning of an awareness of how human activity affected the environment, of the growing danger of toxic chemicals that *Silent Spring* author Rachel Carson had written about. We would educate and inform the public about our mission.

I had another close call when I was able to corral a US Forest Service plane to fly over California's Sierra Nevada Mountains to photograph and document the conditions at solid waste sites so I could produce a slide show on solid waste management. The pilot was an Alaskan bush pilot who told me he had recently flown some Russian scientists throughout Alaska, so I felt reasonably confident he would have the skills of a bush pilot to transport me into some less accessible Sierra Nevada Mountain sites.

The EPA was concerned about a solid waste dump site possibly contaminating Lake Almanor, a Pacific Gas & Electric reservoir on a tributary of the Feather River that provided hydroelectric power to Californians. A Pacific storm front had just arrived as we took off from the lakeside landing strip to return, which was above 10,000 feet in the mid-northern Sierras. Reports said we might encounter baseball-size hail stones if we flew directly back to the Bay Area, so the pilot took the only possible escape route to the east.

This pilot proved to me he had to be one of the best to fly in Alaska. The clouds had closed in, and the only exit was to skim barely feet above the water, aiming for a notch in the surrounding peaks at the east end of the lake that had very little clearance. I held my breath as we squeezed through the notch and were suddenly overlooking the vast Nevada desert. "That's Reno in the distance where we can land until the storm passes," he said. I was sure we had avoided certain disaster.

Reducing Smog and the Arab Oil Embargo

There was not much awareness about the environmental degradation that was happening in the San Francisco Bay area where I lived, or even Los Angeles, where smog alerts were now a regular occurrence. The automobile was king of the road. Transit and trolley lines had almost disappeared except for the cable cars that gave that scenic ride over Nob Hill to North Beach and Fisherman's Wharf, or that connected Market Street to Golden Gate Park. They were mostly for the tourists.

We held many hearings on what had to be done to mitigate the growing air pollution and how legislation could cure the growing smog problem that was damaging the lungs of school children in metropolitan areas like the San Francisco Bay area, the Sacramento and San Joaquin Valleys, and Los Angeles. All were enclosed in geographic basins that allowed the ingredients of smog to accumulate to dangerous levels, particularly when trapped under inversion layers on hot days. The smog was largely caused by motor vehicles that produced some 80 percent of the air pollution at the time.

Here was a chance to lobby for decreased use of fossil fuels that the Clean Air Act required for the reduction of air pollution. The EPA already had a fleet of Liquid Natural Gas-fueled cars in their LA carpool, but driving one was like driving a bumper-car. One could push the gas pedal to the floor with very little response. "Big deal," I thought at the time. "Is this the best we can do to lower auto emissions?"

During the 1973 Arab Israeli War, Arab members of the Organization of Petroleum Exporting Countries (OPEC) imposed an embargo on oil exports to the United States and some other European countries in retaliation for the US decision to re-supply the Israeli military. It was to gain leverage in the post-war peace negotiations over ownership of the Suez Canal.

This resulted in long lines of cars waiting at gas stations for a tank of gas. Those gas stations frequently ran out of their supply, which in turn triggered several recessions and raging inflation because the American economy was so dependent on oil and gas.

The long lines at gas stations caused by the Arab oil embargos of 1973 had gotten the public's attention. It also had the attention of the EPA who thought that fewer vehicles on the road during the embargo was an opportunity to "sell" the newly-enacted Clean Air Act to Californians by proposing gas rationing as one of the remedies to mitigate the high smog levels until smog levels in general were brought under control.

It was just one of the many proposals to implement the Clean Air Act that focused largely on land use and transportation. Also included were increased parking fees, carpool lanes on freeways, land use controls to prevent sprawl, and catalyst retrofits for cars built in 1966 -74.

The EPA's Office of General Counsel in Washington, DC, reviewed the draft plan and found that it was still insufficient to meet the law's tight attainment deadlines. To reach attainment, they added a regulation to cut gasoline use in the area by 86%

with gas rationing from May through October, the annual "smog season", starting in 1975.

I was commissioned to make a film about the possibility of gas rationing during the Arab oil embargo. Francis Ford Coppola, the Hollywood director of Oscar-winning films such as *The Godfather* and *Apocalypse Now,* had moved his filmmaking headquarters to the Bay Area. I was able to edit the film at his American Zoetrope Studio in San Francisco because we had no in-house film or photography studio facilities.

Coppola was a very supportive and generous man when it came to fighting the good fights and was happy to work with us to grow public awareness of the need to protect the environment.

The film, entitled *The Great Clean Air Debate*, was built around the gas ration hearings in Los Angeles and pictures of the smog-filled LA Basin. Folksinger Don McLean gave us permission to use his song *Tapestry* in the soundtrack, a song about the evils of pollution. His most famous song at that time was *Bye, Bye, Miss American Pie*, but *Tapestry* better articulated the harm of polluted water and air. In his own right, McLean also spent much of his time with Pete Seeger on his Hudson River cruises that resulted in the cleanup of that waterway.

Tapestry

Every thread of creation is held in position
by still other strands of things living.
In an earthly tapestry hung from the skyline

of smouldering cities so gray and so vulgar,
as not to be satisfied with their own negativity
but needing to touch all the living as well.

Every breeze that blows kindly is one crystal breath
we exhale on the blue diamond heaven.
As gentle to touch as the hands of the healer.
As soft as farewells whispered over the coffin.
We're poisoned by venom with each breath we take,
from the brown sulphur chimney and the black
highway snake.

Every fish that swims silent, every bird that flies
freely,
every doe that steps softly.
Every crisp leaf that falls, all the flowers that grow
on this colorful tapestry, somehow they know.
That if man is allowed to destroy all they need.
He will soon have to pay with his life, for his greed.

The *Great Clean Air Debate* included footage of much of the California Air Resources Board hearings in Los Angeles to enforce the Clean Air Act. With everyone dependent on cars to commute to work, how would the EPA be able to convince Los Angelenos? The local Chambers of Commerce rebelled against any ordinance that even implied gas rationing. They threatened in the hearings that up to half a million Los Angelenos could lose their jobs, and those who had jobs would have difficulty getting to work. The California Air Resources Board lost that round. The Los Angeles City Council refused to institute even a mild form of gas rationing.

In fact, Los Angelenos had few transportation alternatives. They were paying a price for the disappearance of the Los Angeles trolleys. The Pacific Electric Company Red Line was the last of them connecting downtown LA with San Pedro and Port of Los Angeles, the largest harbor and a major economic driver on the West Coast.

A transportation company partially owned by General Motors and Goodyear Tire Company bought the Red Line from the city and tore up the tracks, replacing the trolleys with diesel-powered buses by 1961. We at the EPA thought it incredible that Los Angeles could be so short-sighted about the loss of their trolleys, and its impact on their future transportation needs. Of equal concern was the air pollution resulting from gasoline engine use that caused schools to close on second-stage smog alerts when ozone levels were highest.

Then and Now

It is a different world today, some 50 years later, thanks to the regulations implemented by the Environmental Protection Agency. Los Angeles woke up to the fact that it needed a modern transportation system. Its modern streetcar system includes the Metro Blue Line (opened in 1990), the Metro Red Line (1993), the Metro Green Line (1995), the resurrection of the Pacific Electric Red Car Trolley at the Port of Los Angeles (2003), the Metro Gold Line (2004) and the Gold Line Extension (2009), and the anticipated opening of the Expo Line to West LA and the Westside Subway Extension.

The EPA was empowered to provide startup funds and help organize clean air forums under the Clean Air Act. A co-worker and I delivered a $2,000 check from the EPA to the Los Angeles Region Tuberculosis and Respiratory Disease Association to jump start the first Santa Monica Clean Air Convention. The Santa Monica Civic Auditorium was an ideal location and is still a showcase for the latest technologies that mitigate air pollution.

Today the Santa Monica Clean Air Convention has morphed into the AltCar Expo, "the nation's leading forum for green car ride and drive, public education and demonstration of the latest green technology vehicles," according to a recent press release. "AltCar Expo will present the most extensive array of sustainable vehicles in one place, including: electric, plugin hybrid electric, natural gas, propane, biodiesel, ethanol and hydrogen vehicles." It's good to know our efforts have grown into the strong environmental movement and regulations we have today.

The USEPA Western Regional Office in San Francisco is now housed in a skyscraper, with 738 employees enforcing the laws and regulations governing all pollutants and hazardous chemicals including greenhouse gases such as carbon dioxide, now the major cause of the atmospheric overheating that is melting the polar icecaps at an alarming rate.

There are still the challenges from more western wildfires, the increasing frequency of droughts, devastating hurricanes, and water levels rising in coastal cities such as Miami. Internationally, it must fight to fulfill the Paris Accord in which 199 nations say they will work to keep earth temperatures from rising more than two percent centigrade. We are already seeing the results of climate change: the record droughts in Africa and the Middle East that are causing so much geopolitical unrest, civil wars, and the migration of millions of refugees to Europe.

There are many more opportunities to take up the fight to uphold our environmental standards, as worsening environmental conditions make it more difficult to ignore the costs and consequences of ignorance.

My time with the EPA ended when the 18-month contract had expired. To remain longer I would have had to become a civil servant, and several returned veterans with similar qualifications had higher civil service ratings because of their service in Vietnam, so they had priority over me.

I moved to Los Angeles hoping to find more film work. I had a cousin who was committed to César Chávez and the United Farmworkers Union's cause. Cousin John also belonged to the Los Angeles Chapter of the AFL-CIO Labor Council, so when César asked for assistance from his fellow unions to rehabilitate and modernize the new UFW Headquarter at La Paz, I began accompanying him to see what the United Farmworkers Union of America was all about.

Chapter Seven

César Chávez and the United Farmworkers Union

of America

John was a pro-union carpenter and building designer who had been renovating the new United Farmworkers headquarters at La Paz in Keene, California, for almost a year. It was a 200-acre former tuberculosis sanitorium beside a small railroad maintenance yard on the road from Bakersfield to Tehachapi.

I had heard of the United Farmworkers Union several years earlier while working as a television news cameraman for KTTV Channel 11, a Sacramento TV station.

One shoot was a weekend special report on the US Immigration Service in action to show their prowess in protecting the borders. We reported on the Immigration Service rounding up undocumented aliens in the fields—Mexican and Central American seasonal workers—while they were working.

I thought then it was an unjust system, as I filmed these so-called "illegals" being chased down and herded like cattle by "La Migra", their term for the Immigration Service. The growers, of course, knew many of the workers did not have valid Green Card work visas and had turned a blind eye to the labor contractors that smuggled them across the border.

I learned much about California labor relations while filming for KTTV and watching how the growers operated. Farm workers had almost no protections in those days, since even those with legal work visas weren't given adequate housing or benefits. It was a brutal system, so when Cousin John asked if I wanted to help him out with whatever needed to be done in La Paz to support the United Farmworkers Union, I thought it a worthy cause. I had little idea of what that meant at the time even though I had worked with farmworkers in a Turkish village as a Peace Corps Volunteer for two years.

It was easy to see that the UFW needed lots of help. I met César Chávez at a low point in the UFW. La Paz had a small staff for several reasons. The United Farmworkers Union had just 6,000 members. This was after many growers had signed Teamster 'sweetheart' contracts to avoid re-signing expired UFW labor contracts. Its membership was as high as 70,000 in the early 1970s.

César had purchased the former Kern County TB sanitorium in 1971 that had been abandoned when modern wonder drugs made the quarantine of TB patients no longer necessary. The UFW had outgrown its original Delano headquarters in the San Joaquin valley as union membership grew.

Re-named Nuestra Senora Reina de la Paz, or Our Lady Queen of Peace, it contained dormitories for the farmworkers and staff who worked there. The former sanitorium was leased from Edward Lewis, a Hollywood film producer who supported many social causes. He had to be the straw buyer of record of La Paz from its Kern County owners, since Kern County's decision-makers were no friend to the UFW.

There was a lot of work to be done at La Paz to make it habitable for farmworkers and staff. Cousin John had already begun to renovate the dormitories to house farmworkers and staff, as well as modernize the hospital. The place had been abandoned for years, and since I had worked as a carpenter several summers to pay for my UC education, I was happy to assist.

I soon began spending weeks instead of weekends at La Paz, and hoped I would have the opportunity to use my film and photography skills as I did with the Environmental Protection Agency, since this was a chance to record history in the making. It seemed to be a call to work in another new frontier that President Kennedy had spoken of, advancing human rights using peaceful means to better farmworkers' lives.

So, I became a fulltime resident of La Paz in January 1974, whereas Cousin John still lived and worked in Los Angeles.

But he could be called upon to bring up any necessary skilled labor. In fact, without the skilled union carpenters, plumbers, plasterers and electricians John was always bringing from Los Angeles, César couldn't have completed the Agbayani Retirement Village for retired Filipino farmworkers. He wanted to honor them because they were the first to strike for better working conditions and join the UFW. He said many times

Agbayani Village was an example of benefits that would be possible for UFW members.

The Strikes

The Teamsters Union was already in the grape vineyards there because they had organized the cannery and transportation workers and were willing to weaken their more democratic UFW union brothers and sisters in any way they could.

Many of the vegetable growers in the Salinas and San Joaquin valleys had signed five-year agreements that excluded limits on exposure to pesticides and certain hiring policies or grievance procedures that UFW members had won. The Teamster contracts did not have a union hiring hall that gave precedence to those out of work, or paid unemployment insurance when there was no longer work that year—which union farmworkers had also enjoyed with the UFW.

Workers were told they had to sign Teamster Labor Contracts in 10 days or risk being fired. Moreover, the contracts increased wages by a meager five cents on the piece rate annually, which was based on the quantity picked rather than hourly wages, according to Jerry Cohen, the UFW's chief counsel at the time.

The Teamsters were therefore able to sign labor contracts with more than 375 California growers. Teamster's President Frank Fitzsimmons had allied the Teamsters with President Nixon and California Governor Ronald Reagan—both supporters of the growers who had resisted any effort to apply the National Labor Relations Act to farmworkers, which would have given the UFW more protections again unlawful organizing tactics and working conditions.

That sparked a bitter months-long strike by grape workers in California's Coachella and San Joaquin valleys. Some 3,500 nonviolent strikers were arrested for violating anti-picketing injunctions, many of which were later overturned as unconstitutional. Hundreds of strikers were beaten, dozens were shot and two were murdered.

Nixon had a history of opposing labor unions wherever and whenever he could. He in fact won his first congressional race by opposing and red-baiting Congresswoman Helen Gahagan Douglas during the McCarthy era. She was a liberal Democrat from southern California and the wife of Hollywood actor Melvyn Douglas.

All Nixon had to do during the anti-communist insanity of the McCarthy era was hint that favoring labor unions was in fact favoring socialism, one of the scare words that tarred so many during Hollywood's blacklist days, an era that I witnessed firsthand when I returned to Los Angeles and to work in Hollywood.

It was piecework all over again with the Teamster's sweetheart contracts—no latrine breaks, or hourly pay, overtime, or pensions. All the UFW could do was hit the growers in the pocketbook, and the lettuce and grape boycotts were born. César never forgave the Teamsters for turning against their Farmworker Union brothers and sisters, even after they had settled their differences several years later.

UFW History

Organizing California farmworkers had a long history even before César's organizing efforts. The community development principles that I had learned in the Peace Corps came from union organizing efforts in the 1930s during the Great Depression. And César had studied them, which helped me to understand him.

Most labor organizers had learned from Saul Alinsky who first developed the principles of labor organizing. He wrote about his work organizing industrial workers in Chicago in his most famous book, *Rules for Radicals*[1], which was really about the rules for successfully negotiating labor contracts with employers.

His rules were hardly radical, but a study of what brought communities together to achieve common goals. The British were already using community development principles to assist in their colonies' independence movements by selecting community leaders and stakeholders to facilitate their economic development, those same principles taught to Peace Corps Volunteers that enabled my successes in a Turkish village.

It was community development work all over again, and I stepped in wherever I was needed when not in the fields recording events, happy to be part of such a movement to better lives.

César first came to Delano in the San Joaquin Valley of California to organize what was originally called the United Farmworkers Organizing Committee. César loved to talk

---

[1] Alinsky, Saul David. *Rules for radicals: A practical primer for realistic radicals*. Vintage, 1989.

about those early days of "La Huelga", the Spanish word for struggle. One famous anecdote was about United Auto Workers President Walter Reuther who had dropped in for a visit during the earliest years of their organizing efforts while farmworkers were picketing a line of refrigerated rail cars to convince other farmworkers not to load them with non-union picked lettuce. When the police arrived to arrest them for breaking the all-too-frequent court injunctions to prevent farmworkers from picketing, they stopped taking names when Walter Reuther identified himself. The police said they didn't dare arrest such a famous man and left the scene rather than book anyone.

Chávez was aided by many others, including other union leaders like United Auto Workers Paul Schrade, President of the Los Angeles UAW office, who was later wounded by the same gun that killed Bobby Kennedy in the Roosevelt Hotel. It was his support, as well as new UAW President Leonard Woodcock in 1974, that continued to provide financial aid with $10,000 checks each month.

The UFW never had it easy due to the growers' opposition to a farmworkers union, and Teamster Union efforts to break the UFW. Without the cash infusions from the AFL-CIO and United Auto Workers, there wasn't enough money to pay staff—which was $10 per week, $15 if we were on the road. The AFL-CIO Council had donated $1.5 million to the United Farmworkers of America in 1973 to keep the UFW afloat. It was difficult for us, the staff, to keep up our morale during those times.

But it didn't discourage César, who was part cheerleader, fundraiser, publicist—all requirements of the great union leaders that he wanted to emulate. He had become the leader of a social movement, a movement espoused by the American Catholic Church, dealing with barely educated farmworkers who spoke little or no English. That made it a spiritual movement as well, which is why so many farmworkers believed in him. It was the struggle for "La Causa", the struggle for equality of pay and benefits, as well as justice in the courts.

I saw how the farmworkers worshipped him as the leader of their struggle for basic rights when I followed and filmed him talking to them in the fields. He had tremendous charisma, with coal dark eyes that would search your very soul for the level of commitment to "La Causa". In many cases it was the women who would push their men to go on strike. Dolores Huerta cofounded the UFW with Chávez for that reason. She was regarded as "La Passionara", the passionate heart of their cause for greater justice. I saw it as worthy as my Peace Corps years in bettering lives.

César was dark-skinned because he was part Indian. He never tired of telling us how his family had lost their Arizona farm during the Great Depression. Organizing a farmworkers union became a cause for workers' rights, their rights to bargain for higher wages and benefits. Many farmworkers were undocumented in those days, as I said, which made it easier for growers to exploit them.

It was difficult to describe how the farmworkers felt in ordinary words, so I wrote several poems to describe what I saw firsthand. *The Farmworker's Prayer* describes a moment I witnessed that captures just how much Mexican farmworkers worshipped César during one of the marches through Coachella Valley as farmworkers were still in the fields harvesting, on a warm, twilit evening.

The Farmworker's Prayer

It was already dusk,

When César Chávez,

President of his Union,

Walked beside a field,

Like many he had worked in.

Others followed with blood red flags,

Flying Black Aztec Eagles,

That led their march from piecework,

Short hoes,

And extreme poverty.

Among shapes barely visible

Under still warm stars,

A woman with kerchief-wrapped hair,

And heavy gloves,

Suddenly appeared.

Kneeling,

She sang her poem

To the greatness of César,

Who like Christ,

Had led her people.

Was it blasphemy

To so honor one man?

But César pulled her up

to return her tribute,

With his own.

It was the women,

Who first struck, he said,

Who prodded their men to rise up

From the muddy fields,

To a better destiny.

Who else could so move a man,

With the hopes of their children?

Chapter Eight

Surviving with the UFW Boycotts

La Paz looked empty when I joined the UFW. This was in part because César had staffed boycott offices in various cities to both raise funds and picket supermarket chains to urge consumers to boycott those stores that didn't sell UFW-harvested lettuce and grapes.

It was a struggle for survival with the UFW, having lost so many members. With just a small staff still at La Paz, we had to put our hearts and minds into the struggle for the UFW to survive. The Teamsters Union was doing its best to bankrupt us at the time by also using Teamster goon squads brought up from Southern California to violently attack UFW picket lines in the field.

César spoke often of Martin Luther King, Jr.'s use of non-violent protest in picketing workers to publicize their cause and recruit new members. The fight for greater farmworkers' rights was a recognition that seasonal agricultural workers had almost no rights. In response to the violence perpetrated by Teamster goon squads, César called off the strike and began a second grape boycott. Once again, strikers, union staff and volunteers spread out to cities across North America, organizing popular support for the boycotts of table grapes, lettuce and Gallo wine.

These boycotts were the only way the UFW could fight back against the Teamsters' sweetheart contracts and bring national attention to their conditions. It was a call for consumers to buy only UFW-picked produce sold in grocery stores and markets. With the support of Bobby and Ethel Kennedy and Martin Luther King, Jr.'s widow to help publicize their efforts, these boycotts succeeded in bringing more socially-conscious supermarket chains to sell only UFW produce.

It wasn't until 1977 that the Teamsters union agreed to sign a historic "jurisdictional" agreement with the UFW and leave the fields. In 1978, the UFW called off its boycotts of grapes, lettuce and Gallo wines when the California Labor Relations law took full effect and enshrined into law the right of farmworkers to strike and vote for union membership.

The grape and lettuce boycotts were coordinated by Anna Puharich, Director of the UFW Service Center, who had set up boycott offices in 12 cities to also solicit food donations and funds to support the UFW and feed those of us as well at La Paz during the low point in membership.

The Service Center was set up as a non-profit organization to operate the UFW properties, including the health clinics that served the health needs of the farmworkers. César wanted a separate entity to own and maintain union facilities so as not to interfere with their union organizing efforts.

I worked under Anna, which enabled me to film and record union activities as the head of the newly formed UFW Film Department.

Anna's "takeover" of the Service Center was not without controversy among some of the social activists. She was a New York society matron from, in their eyes, the liberal, wealthy elites, but that is what the UFW needed at that time. It couldn't have survived without the monies and shipments of food that we and the farmworkers on strike needed, literally, to survive.

On the Picket Lines

I felt privileged to be part of what had become a social movement when accompanying César on his organizing trips to where the farmworkers lived. Many were in "La Colonias" as they were called: usually segregated Hispanic communities near the fields. César was the skilled community organizer always on the move to recruit more union members, coordinate a strike, or visit the boycott cities to publicize, the farmworkers' struggle for social and economic justice.

We always caravanned through California and Arizona in a column of the UFW's Plymouth Valiants. They all had what were called "slant six" engines, six-cylinder engines that were mounted at an angle to fit under the hood. Because they were identical models, anyone who meant to harm César would not know which car held him. We would know which Plymouth carried him because of the orange-colored windshield rear-view mirror. Plymouths were easily maintained and the parts interchangeable by UFW mechanics in our La Paz garage, which made them easy to service. Those of us travelling with César were meant to be part of a protective shield. We carefully chose the safest travel routes and always maintained the 55 mile-per-hour speed limit of those days, so police would have no excuse to harass or stop us.

I also began to contribute to the UFW newspaper *El Malcriado*, which loosely meant 'The Naughty Boy'. It was an incredible bi-monthly information source that kept up our spirits during those desperate times for the UFW.

César was tough on his staff. He fired Carlos, its talented editor at that time, when he discovered that Carlos was expensing some of his scarce *El Malcriado* budget to pay for his pet's dog food. That was on top of a personal expense budget that was just $10 per week—$15 if we were traveling—and César was merciless in accounting for every scarce dollar the UFW had at what was the scarcest of times.

El Malcriado was distributed monthly in those days to every corner of California, Arizona, and even Texas where the UFW had a small presence. Its inspirational stories rallied farmworkers with the latest news and fiery speeches by César, Dolores Huerta, co-founder of the UFW, and the labor organizers in the field who actually led the strikes.

That was how the UFW was regarded in those days. The growers resisted any organizing effort that bettered the lives of their farmworkers, preferring to rely on labor contractors to keep their pay as low as possible with no benefits. Many of the contractors were the same coyotes that smuggled undocumented workers across the border. I remember my film crew of two (me with camera and a sound man recording) being accompanied out of several towns with a police car in the next lane. The local police would harass us in any way they could—giving parking tickets, even once citing a faulty muffler in Oxnard during the strawberry strike. I almost lost my driver's license because of the many citations.

My film crew, armed with a professional 16 mm Éclair hand-held camera and sound recorder, prevented some arrests and harassment by local police and Deputy Sheriffs by filming the strikes, because we would sometimes be mistaken for a local TV crew.

I was called to one picket line where the UFW was attempting to organize Oxnard strawberry pickers in Southern California working in one of California's largest strawberry fields. My sound man and I arrived just as police in riot gear were coming off their bus to arrest the UFW picketers that were defying a court injunction against picketing in Oxnard's strawberry fields. UFW picketers always lined up on the edge of access roads while urging the strawberry pickers to come out of the fields and join the strike.

The police were in full riot gear, wearing plastic visors, flak vests, and carrying wooden batons. A police helicopter hovered overhead, as if to document the illegal picketing. But the moment we began filming, the police climbed back on the bus and disappeared, as did the helicopter.

It was obvious the police didn't want any adverse publicity. We were about to publicize the arrest of dozens of farmworkers who were exercising their right to picket and organize other farmworkers.

The publicity was so important that César even launched a protest march out of the Oxnard La Colonia during that same strawberry strike. It was a small and well-kept village adjacent to the fields where many of the farmworkers lived. He paraded the farmworkers through its streets and into the fields to protest the injunction again picketing, which I, and other journalists, covered. It was a grand occasion with hundreds of farmworkers holding UFW flags as they marched through the streets of La Colonia. César knew how to put on a show.

César received many death threats, which is why we took so many precautions when he traveled. German-trained German Shepherds guarded him. They were housed in kennels at UFW Headquarters. Red was his favorite, a giant and fearsome looking German Shepherd with a brown-red coat that accompanied César whenever possible on parades, speeches, and the like. These highly trained guard dogs lived just seven to ten years because they were so highly bred. It was a sad day when Red died during my year and was buried with much ceremony at La Paz.

Life at La Paz was peaceful when we weren't visiting picket lines or the dozen Service Center health clinics set up by the UFW to maintain farm workers' health. Nuestra Senora Reina de La Paz's relative isolation made it a quiet place of refuge. I could see why César had chosen it, though César's wife Helen and their eight children wouldn't move to Keene for the first six months because she had been quarantined there as a child with tuberculosis. Many farmworker children suffered from TB in those days because of their primitive living conditions before modern wonder drugs abolished the need for sanitoriums.

One of César's legs was shorter than the other, causing his spinal column to fuse, according to his doctor. He would collapse at times in extreme pain. But when healthy, he would challenge us to a quick hike up a hill behind La Paz. I was 33 years old at the time and had difficulty keeping up.

I remember at staff meetings César would say he yearned for the time he could retire as President of the United Farmworkers of America, such as other union presidents were doing. He said he especially admired and wanted to emulate the International Brotherhood of Electrical Workers. The IBEW is still one of the strongest and most democratic trade unions still controlled by its members.

Though we spent most of our time filming and reporting on the picket lines throughout the Salinas, San Joaquin, Coachella, and Imperial Valleys where so much of California's produce was grown, it was in Arizona that the UFW had the most problem organizing farmworkers.

Chapter Nine

The Yuma Citrus Strike

It was called the Yuma, Arizona, Citrus Strike by the public media and attracted national attention because Yuma was the center of a very large citrus growing region populated with large lemon and grapefruit groves.

The Yuma Strike almost bankrupted the UFW, in part because the border with Mexico was porous. The Colorado River that formed part of the border was so shallow where it crossed into Mexico that strikebreakers could wade across it easily. So, César's cousin Manuel Chávez, who was head of union organizing in the south, attempted to blockade the Mexican border at San Luis, a small village at the Mexican border.

The strike was called in the extreme heat and humidity of August 1974 against lemon growers in the Yuma orchards, and within a couple of weeks 1,500 farmworkers were on strike. I didn't arrive to report on it for *El Malcriado* until September. Manuel began paying strike benefits of $50 a week. The growers tried to recruit strikebreakers, but without much luck. Hardly anyone but an experienced desert Limosnero, as they were called, could put up with a day's work in the August heat of the

Yuma Valley, and the UFW was able to keep the 1,500 striking Limosneros during the harvest season.

But it wasn't enough. The growers were able to smuggle strikebreakers across the porous border. There were plenty willing to work. Although San Luis, Arizona, had maybe 2,000 residents, San Luis, Mexico, across the border, was a large city of almost 50,000 separated by a poorly patrolled and maintained chain link and barbed wire fence that stretched out across the desert.

The UFW attempted to blockade it for approximately five miles with a string of large army tents set up within 50 feet of the border at approximately quarter-mile intervals in a line stretching east of San Luis. Using dune buggies, cars, vans, and small trucks, the striking farmworkers would chase people attempting to cross. The "road" along the US border was really a sand track that bogged down most vehicles in softer spots, which made the pursuit difficult.

I also began to document what Manuel had set up across the border. He had convinced the Mexican Municipal Police to pick up those who were crossing the border at night before they even crossed. One popular crossover point was several miles outside of the town near a cemetery where the border fence was just three strands of barbed wire. It was an older cemetery with cast iron fencing, I remember. The police would wait on the back side in the darkness. When a carload of strikebreakers was dropped off to cross the border there, the "Municipales", as they were called, would swoop in and arrest them, then cart them back to a large, vacant building opposite the Police Station, where they were held overnight before being released.

It was literally a catch and release operation, and ultimately a failure when Mexican President Luis Echeverria got involved, which happened later in the story.

I was on one such nighttime foray with my camera when the Federales, the Mexican National Police, stopped us and stuck an automatic weapon through the car window while asking what we were doing on a road that ended at the Colorado River. The driver told them it was to report on the strike for the American public. That explanation seemed to satisfy the Federales who then let us continue.

During the day, we also had a small plane to track strikers and strikebreakers from the air piloted by a San Diego Catholic priest. I could hitch a ride in his plane to film the strike from the air. Father Joe was a very experienced pilot, though I held my breath every time he took off and landed on that same sandy landing strip beside the border.

It was a badly timed lemon strike. For starters, the monies were running out as the growers wouldn't settle, even though it was the height of the picking season. The 18,000 acres of lemon orchards sat on a mesa that ran for some 26 miles from the San Luis Rio Colorado north to Yuma, where California, Mexico, and Arizona came together. It was too huge an area for the strike to cover.

Most of the field workers lived in San Luis, Sonora, and crossed the border every day either with regular work permits or resident alien green cards. Some crossed at the beginning of the harvest season and lived in labor camps strung between Yuma and the border. Others lived in makeshift camps in the orchards.

The strikebreakers even stepped through holes in the chain link fence near downtown San Luis, Sonora, or walked a few hundred yards east into the desert, where the fence became three strands of barbed wire strung between posts. It was too easy to break the blockade, in other words.

The union was also spending more money there than anywhere else that year—eventually the strike cost the union $1,235,580.87, according to later newspaper accounts. César called for a rally and news conference in San Luis to publicize the strike and encourage those on strike. It was his first appearance since returning from a trip to Europe. I was there, along with some 700 people attending the rally.

But César couldn't speak to the waiting crowd. He was in such pain from his curved spine that he had to remain in the hotel room. We journalists were clustered around his bed in that tiny motel room as he gave his news conference grimacing in pain as he spoke. He told us that if the lemon growers wouldn't agree to talk, the union might have to return to a boycott.

He was in bed, he said, "because I'm one of those ten percent of people who have one leg shorter than the other. It's the same problem President Kennedy had."

César finally asked Service Center Director Anna Puharich to travel to San Luis to personally supervise the strike and become the Friday morning paymaster to stem the hemorrhaging of

UFW funds. The strike was over in three months, because the harvest was over. The growers had waited the strikers out, rather than sign union contracts.

Another union back breaker was the actions of then Mexican President Luis Echeverria, who ultimately put a stop to the "wet line" (named for the border blockade of "wetbacks" during the UFW's Yuma strike) by ordering the Mexican Army to patrol the Mexican boundary roads to make sure there would be no attempts to prevent Mexican citizens from crossing the Arizona border, either legally or illegally. He said it was the constitutional right of every Mexican citizen to travel wherever they wanted, and such a right could never be restricted.

The Yuma Citrus Strike was one of the UFW's greatest failures. But cousin Manuel had kept organizing rallies in California's Imperial and Coachella Valleys, where his efforts were more successful in firing up his base. It had been their land originally, after all. I attended several of his rallies and wrote this poem to describe Manuel's charisma in rallying farmworkers to "La Huelga", as he called it.

Viva La Huelga

"Long live the strike!"

Cried Manuel Chávez,

The Union's field organizer,

César's cousin.

As chief rabble-rouser.

He spoke in staccato

Bursts of emotion,

His hands flashed the message

That victory was near,

To the farmworker's tightly-packed faces,

Uplifted with tears.

Coachella, Calexico, and border Mexico,

Heard his call,

Even the citrus groves of Yuma and San Luis

Let fruit fall,

While the Colorado trickled,

Around their ankles,

Who waded across,

And eluded pursuit.

Victory will be ours, he chanted,

As this land once was ours.

Let us support each other,

Starve the growers,

As we have starved,

Multiply so we may prosper,

That we may claim once more,

That for which

Our ancestors have suffered!

The Calexico Funeral

César was brilliant at publicizing farmworker conditions and took advantage of another tragedy to make national news. He had me film and photograph the funeral ceremony for that reason.

Forty-five farmworkers were being driven to work before dawn near Blythe, California, in the Imperial Valley that same winter. The bus driver was either drowsy or driving too fast and missed a 90-degree turn in the darkness after the 100-mile, two-hour drive, plunging off the embankment that bordered an 18-foot-deep irrigation canal. Nineteen of the 45 farm workers on the bus were trapped in 10 feet of water unable to escape in the darkness, with many crushed from the impact.

César then organized a funeral and marched 19 caskets that accounted for the dead farmworkers across the Calexico border to a Mexicali cemetery on Avenida Francisco Madera where the drowned victims were buried. It was a magnificent procession with crowds lining the way into Mexico, the borders wide open to let them through.

The Bishop of Baja, California, first gave them a very impressive and special mass and benediction in Calexico's National Guard Armory before 1,000 mourners, caskets draped with the Aztec eagle, the UFW flag.

It was an incredibly moving sight, as if they were being honored as veterans returned from a war. Few knew at the time that some of those caskets were empty. Many of the bodies had already been taken to the homes of families in Mexico to be mourned. But it was important that 19 caskets crossed the border to commemorate and honor all of them.

The labor contractor who owned the bus, Jesus Ayala, was a well-known scab herder and strikebreaker, said a newspaper description of the accident. The *Yuma Sun* reported:

> The driver, fifty-five-year-old Pablo Navarro Arellano, was in the midst of an eighteen-hour workday when the accident occurred. Typically, his job began at two a.m., when he went to the enormous shape-up at el hoyo, the hole, in Calexico, picked up the workers, and then drove about 130 miles to the farm. There he supervised the lettuce thinning for ten hours, drove back to el hoyo, dropped off the workers, cleaned out the bus, and finally left for home and a few hours' sleep. The lettuce thinners were paid nothing for

the four hours' travel time between the hole and High and Mighty Farms.

"This tragedy happened because of the greed of the big growers who do not care about the safety of the workers and expose them to grave dangers when they transport them in wheeled coffins to the fields," UFW leader César Chávez told the crowd, according to a commentary he published in the *Los Angeles Times* in 1974.[1]

This poem better describes what we felt witnessing it.

The Drowned Bus

The nineteen farmworkers

Still looked asleep,

As their bus rose slowly,

Windows streaming water,

Pulled from the irrigation ditch.

Most had been dozing

From the border crossing,

That early morning,

To harvest before sunrise

Penetrated the fields too deeply.

---

[1] https://www.latimes.com/archives/lapm-1999-aug-27-me-4246- story.html

Only such sweat,

From the irrigated desert,

Brought melons and strawberries,

To our breakfast tables,

Cool and ready to eat.

They picked what was ripe,

Quit every hot afternoon,

Until their driver,

Dazed by sleepless nights,

Missed his turn.

Those nineteen coffins,

Returned to their casas,

Draped with Aztec eagles

Was such a grand event,

When blessed by Baja's Bishop.

The snakelike procession slowly

Wound its writhing way

Across the Mexican border that day,

Carrying hissing eagles on its back,

No green cards were needed,

For those now liberated from their past.

Chapter Ten

Parting Ways

Times were desperate for the UFW. It made for an incredible year for me, not only in filming and reporting on union activities and the boycott that literally fed us during the winter of 1974, but for building up a library of films and photos in the UFW Service Center that could be reviewed by anyone interested in its history.

I had located an earlier history of the farmworkers' movement while acting as head of the Service Center's Film Department. It was a copy of a banned documentary, *Poverty in The Valley of Plenty,* from the storied Southern Poverty Law Center, headquartered in Montgomery, Alabama. The Center was founded in 1971 in the aftermath of the civil rights movement to archive any materials pertaining to labor struggles as well as "to ensure that the promise of the civil rights movement became a reality for all."

The film had been banned in the 1950s during the McCarthy era, which was also at the beginning of the Hollywood Blacklist, a movement by studio owners to not employ those in the film industry they considered to be members of the Communist Party.

It was ruled to be defamatory in a lawsuit won by DiGiorgio Farms, one of the largest grape growers in the San Joaquin valley. The lawsuit was part of an earlier attempt to stifle a farmworkers union established by the American Federation of Labor Unions. California congressman Richard Nixon was the reported instigator of the DiGiorgio lawsuit that banned the film.

Poverty in The Valley of Plenty was not at all inflammatory. It simply portrayed the plight of farmworkers after WWII who had no ability to bargain for wages and benefits, leaving them open to exploitation by both the growers and labor contractors, just as portrayed in *The Grapes of Wrath*. All copies of *Poverty in the Land of Plenty* had been ordered destroyed by the court, but I was able to screen the Southern Poverty Law Center's copy in La Paz for César and our staff.

The film was produced by the Hollywood Film Council and A.F. of L., which included almost all Hollywood film industry unions, from IATSE, SAG, IBEW, TEAMSTERS, Writers and Producers Guilds, and even the California State Federation of Labor. It was an eerie feeling to see a film about the farmworkers of the 1940s and 1950s, then mostly made up of southern Okies and Blacks with just a sprinkling of Filipinos that were beginning to replace them.

Seeing *Poverty in the Valley of Plenty* probably gave César the idea for the documentary, *Fighting for Our Lives,* one of five films nominated for an Oscar as a feature-length documentary in 1975, after I left the UFW.

It was the end product of a film project that I began with footage from the strikes that I titled *Why We Boycott,* which I had also edited in San Francisco at Francis Ford Coppola's American Zoetrope film studio. César liked the first edit of footage of the strikes I had filmed and asked me to obtain any outtakes from LA area TV stations of the various strikes a year earlier in 1973 that resulted in the deaths of two farmworkers.

We were hoping to find footage of the Teamsters' violent tactics to break up the picket lines, mostly in Kern County and the Coachella Valley. We knew the stories of our non-violent resistance had been effective in drawing out farmworkers to join the strikes. Teamster goons would wait among the grape rows for UFW picketers to appear in the early dawn, then rush at them with baseball bats and grape stakes, injuring many to intimidate and cause them to break from their picket line. But the strikers refused to fight back and held the line. Several local TV stations had filmed the chaotic aftermath as the sun rose.

When I returned to La Paz to show the initial edit of *Why We Boycott,* I was asked for the TV outtakes César had requested. I couldn't answer since I had been in San Francisco editing the rough draft of the film and had not had the time to visit those LA TV stations to collect them.

César promptly put the documentary project in the hands of Reverend Chris Hartmire, who had been the resident Migrant Minister at La Paz in 1973, and who was now living in San Francisco. César had originally wanted us to work together on the film, since Chris was an aspiring filmmaker.

I remember the reason César gave for taking me off the film, which ultimately became *Fighting for Our Lives*. He said he had forgotten a lesson he had learned—never put trust in more than one person in charge of any project. I saw it as César's Achilles heel, his propensity for one-person rule that many believed was the reason for the ultimate demise of UFW membership.

I didn't want to remain much longer with the UFW after César's decision, as much as I admired what we were doing, since as a professional filmmaker with several documentaries to my credit, I wasn't being allowed to complete a work in my chosen profession.

I was close to burnout as well, having recorded some of the UFW history in aiding farmworkers during the UFW's most difficult year as it recovered from the Teamster Union's poaching efforts.

César's last words to me when I announced that I was leaving La Paz at a staff meeting were, "I'll find a Chicano carpenter!" I have no idea why he said that, but it made me realize I was too easily seduced into doing whatever needed to be done with a skeleton staff during the UFW's leanest year.

I had to return to Hollywood if I wanted to continue in my profession.

Chapter Eleven

Building a Livable City

Shortly after returning to Hollywood I learned that *Fighting for Our Lives* had been completed by Glen Pearcy, a producer I had never heard of. Someone on the La Paz staff called me to ask who in Hollywood could nominate it for an Oscar. I suggested Ed Lewis, a friend of the UFW who had purchased La Paz for the UFW because Kern County would not sell La Paz directly to them. He was a noted and prolific Hollywood Producer of such films as *Spartacus, Seven Days in May,* and *Ishi, Last of His Tribe.*

I was happy that *Fighting for Our Lives* was finished and included much of what we had filmed in the past year of strikes. César began showing it as an organizing tool, which helped the UFW win back many of their union grape contracts by the late 1970s.

It was nominated for an Oscar in the Feature Length Documentary category in 1975, but lost to *The Man Who Skied Everest*, a film about a Japanese daredevil's attempt to ski down Mt. Everest. Such were the times, when an adventure film won over a documentary about farm workers' struggles to better their lives.

I wrote several screenplays, acted in TV series, and enjoyed directing plays at Lee Strasberg's Actors Studio when back in Hollywood. But the year in La Paz had made me realize I liked a quieter life than what a future in Hollywood and a filmmaking career could offer.

I had aging parents living in the city of Santa Barbara, so I decided to move closer to them. Santa Barbara was a short distance up the west coast. I hoped for a more stable existence in a place where I could plan my future.

I wanted to be able to contribute to my own community for a change, so I became involved in working to create what architects and planners defined as a "livable" community, a community that protected the environment as well as kept its inhabitants safe. What better place to contribute than where my parents lived who had moved to the area in the 1970s and required more care taking?

My parents lived in an unincorporated area in Santa Barbara County adjacent to the city of Santa Barbara that could use some community planning.

What are the requirements for a livable community? As recently as 2005, the Institute of American Architects said that

> . . . broadly speaking, a livable community
> recognizes its own unique identity and places a
> high value on the planning processes that help

115

manage growth and change to maintain and enhance its community character.

The Goleta Valley still had a rural feeling. It had been settled by immigrant farmers after the Civil War when the huge Spanish rancheros—made up of tens of thousands of acres—were broken up following an especially severe drought that killed the livestock that were the livelihood of the earliest settlers. Now it was a valley filled with lemon and avocado groves.

But a battle had erupted between developers building new subdivisions and environmentalists who wanted to keep the valley as rural and agricultural as possible. The developers had been winning until the environmentalists succeeded in passing a water moratorium that stopped new building projects that didn't have existing water allotments.

I became involved with community events like the Lemon Festival and July 4th celebrations, where I met residents who wanted to live in a unique community. Many of them had already made several attempts to form their own city to control its development.

I thought the Goleta Valley, an area with more than 50,000 inhabitants, should become a city. Its revenues for needed improvements were spent elsewhere in the county rather than for the benefit of the valley. And Goleta continued to attract high tech businesses due to its closeness to the top-ranked physics and engineering schools of the University of California's Santa Barbara campus.

The unplanned expansion had not been preserving the open spaces and pedestrian-friendly commercial centers that residents and sustainable development principles required. The third largest oil spill in U.S. history (behind the Gulf of Mexico and the Alaska oil spills) occurred in the Santa Barbara Channel in 1969. More than three million gallons of crude oil leaked from a deep water well and coated 35 miles of South Coast beaches for months, requiring massive cleanup.

The oil spill mobilized the whole South Coast community, searing the memories of those living there, helping to spawn the national environmental movement.

Goleta had a wonderful history, from its earliest Chumash Indian inhabitants to its discovery in the 1500s by Spanish explorer Juan Cabrillo, which led to the founding of California's mission system. It then became known as "The Good Land", an agricultural paradise named by a local historian for its abundant and fruitful soils and climate.

But as a bedroom community to Santa Barbara, the Goleta Valley had no real community organization of its own other than the Goleta Valley Chamber of Commerce. It needed an established entity to ask for what was needed to improve the valley's aging and dilapidated infrastructure, and to reduce chaotic development. More public transportation, water resources, and just smart community planning were needed to mitigate the effects of a growing population.

There was much opposition to any organizing effort that would create more than a bedroom community in the Goleta

Valley. There were those who wanted to "belong" to the City of Santa Barbara so their property values would be the beneficiary of Santa Barbara property values. They wanted no part of a new, more rural city. Then there were the environmentalists that tended to cluster around UC Santa Barbara with its strong environmental studies program. They were afraid a new city would encourage more development.

But in fact, being unincorporated didn't prevent development: property owners and developers had only to convince one County Supervisor that represented a larger area, rather than a city council responsible for the entire community.

Goletans couldn't agree on what was unique about their own community. Was it a farming culture, bedroom community, or just funky adjunct to UC Santa Barbara? Many thought that, with prosperous Santa Barbara next door, what was the need for another city on the already crowded South Coast? Hence the impasse that had defeated earlier cityhood attempts.

The first step in building a livable community, in my view, had to be creating a town center that could focus planning efforts, and Old Town Goleta seemed just the place to do it. Old Town had been the historical center of the Goleta Valley with stores, a saloon, and a blacksmith for farmers in the early days.

There were marsh lands and the large Goleta slough to the south. Goleta Valley and Santa Barbara have the only southern facing coastlines in California due to a geological quirk. Early schooners could sail into what was then a bay at high tide, refill their water caskets at a natural spring where UC Santa Barbara is now located, and even dock near Old Town's center.

Spanish explorers in the 1700s who were looking for mission sites originally thought it could be an ideal site for a mission, as a large island in the center of the slough had originally held five indigenous Chumash Indian villages and was surrounded by water making it easily defensible. But when the Spaniards returned several years later during a drought, there was very little water to protect it. So, they chose to build the mission in Santa Barbara, which had no natural harbor but a seasonal creek that could provide an adequate water supply.

Old Town, with its own past, could give Goleta Valley residents a sense of their own history and separate community identity. It even had a Community Center that hosted many community activities. The County Planning Director at that time, Dan Gira, also thought Goleta should become a city able to determine its future as part of the County's General Development Plan update.

The update was required by the state of California to accommodate the changes necessitated by a growing population. I was one of many moving to this beautiful area of the South Coast with its unique climate sheltered by east-west mountains and south facing beaches. Santa Barbara and the South Coast has always been a beautiful and very desirable place to live, and the people kept coming.

The County would apply to the state of California for the formation of a Goleta Old Town Redevelopment District, which would allow some tax monies to be withheld for use in Old Town to upgrade its housing and infrastructure. While I loved the beautiful outdoors and the nature that surrounded us, more housing was needed in Old Town. Many Mexican agricultural workers—mostly undocumented—were living in Old Town because of its cheap rents, but landlords were taking advantage by housing ten to twenty of them in a single dilapidated housing unit.

I had to raise $50,000 in the community: 50 percent of the expense the County would incur to do the studies necessary to classify Goleta Old Town as a redevelopment district. Dan Gira and I agreed the County would chip in its 50 percent in the form of time and labor, and whatever was needed for the feasibility study that would determine if Goleta Old Town fulfilled the state requirements for a redevelopment district.

The study would include a report on degraded infrastructure, such as inadequate surface transportation, and the number of bars and other "nonproductive" businesses in Old Town. The point was to determine the extent of blight, or physical deterioration, of the Old Town community, and a cost estimate for fixing those problems.

There was plenty of blight. Goleta's Old Town had become run down in the 1980s as competing malls were built elsewhere to accommodate the new auto-dependent subdivisions built to hold the growing population. Bars had proliferated as businesses left Old Town. A fire partially destroyed a ten-unit apartment building. A Santa Barbara *News-Press* reporter covering the fire reported that residents thought the popping noise from breaking windows sounded like gunfire from gang warfare.

We raised the $50,000, the County Planning Department hired a consultant to write the feasibility study, and it was approved within a year.

Old Town's Revival

Thoughts of forming a new city of Goleta were now revived, and the actual planning of Old Town's future began. There had been several unsuccessful efforts to form a city since the 1970s. The Goleta Old Town Revitalization Committee, a mix of local officials and residents that wanted Old Town's infrastructure and services upgraded, was now created, and I was appointed its chairman. Hearings were held in Old Town's Community building so county planners could learn what Goleta's residents wanted for a future town center. We were following the precepts of community organizing in bringing citizens together to solve some of the problems afflicting such a diverse community.

Goleta in many ways was a microcosm of small-town America and all that had happened to those communities since the sixties: rapid population growth with little concern for the environment. It had an early history combining both rural and urban life with industrial and research centers while being adjacent to the Santa Barbara Airport. I wanted to participate in this organization (that included some future Goleta city mayors), because it could aid in giving the Goleta Valley its "own unique identity" that planners and architects deemed requisite for a livable community.

I had read and was influenced by M. Scott Peck's book *The Different Drum,* describing the elements that bring a community together to achieve whatever they want. His approach epitomized for me the essence of community development. Dr. Peck, a medical doctor, psychologist, and author of a better-known prequel, *The Road Less Traveled,* broke down the steps that a community goes through to come together in a meaningful way in *The Different Drum.*

He warned that the process could take time. Any community usually goes through four stages to reach agreement and to be able to function effectively, whatever its goals. He characterized these stages as Pseudo community, Chaos, Emptiness, and (true) Community.

Pseudo community is the first gathering of any group with the initial pleasantries and avoidance of conflict in the desire to be nice to each other. But it is a false community, because until the second stage of Chaos is reached, individual differences aren't revealed, and a discussion of the real problems doesn't surface.

Chaos described the early stages of our hearings when open discussions brought out the conflict between those residents who loved Old Town's funkiness and cheap rents, and those landlords and landowners who wanted to improve their properties. The goal of the Old Town Advisory Committee was to bring the sides together. There was also a Goleta Beautiful organization that wanted to preserve and restore some of the more historic Old Town structures.

Dr. Peck's third stage is Emptiness: a time of resignation, when the group or organization gives up their individual prejudices, ideologies, control needs, and begins to see what can be accomplished as a group. In Old Town, it wasn't until the second year of the hearings that this happened. More Old Town residents were put on the committee, and we began to see a vision of what a revitalized Old Town could be for the Goleta community.

After many hearings and dialogues with planners, architects, developers, and residents that included a weekend Design Charette that I will discuss in a later chapter, the committee members began to have a sense that we were all in this together and would be able to create something beneficial for the community.

Dr. Peck wrote:

> . . . initially I thought this book's title should be "Peacemaking and Community". But that would put the cart before the horse. For I fail to see how we Americans could effectively communicate with the Russians, (or any peoples of other cultures) when we don't even know how to communicate with the neighbors next door, much less the neighbors on the other side of the tracks.
>
> In our culture of rugged individualism— in which we generally feel that we dare not be honest about ourselves, even with the person in the pew next to us—we bandy around the

word, "community". . . [but] if we are to use the word meaningfully, we must restrict it to a group of individuals who have learned how to communicate honestly with each other.[1]

The Oldtown Revitalization Committee needed two years and 100 hearings to finally form the Old Town Revitalization Plan.

Once the Plan's CEQA (California's Environmental Quality Act) study was approved—a study required to name and mitigate the environmental hazards we might encounter—the County applied to the state of California for the formation of a Goleta Old Town Redevelopment Plan, which would allow a percentage of the tax monies to be withheld for use in Old Town to upgrade its housing, improve San Jose Creek that flowed under its main thoroughfare, and infrastructure.

The final report approved by the County on June 16, 1998, stated: "The purpose and objectives of this Redevelopment Plan are to eliminate the conditions of blight existing in the proposed Project Area and to prevent the recurrence of blighting conditions in said Area."

---

[1] Peck, M. Scott. *The Different Drum.* Simon & Schuster, 1987. P. 56

Chapter Twelve

What Is a Livable City?

We were really wrestling with the concept of what community planners and environmentalists call a "livable city" in our planning effort. That included making neighborhoods safe for children as well as adults.

The population explosion after World War II came to be called the Baby Boom, when a record number of babies were born in the United States. Though born in 1941, I lived through that boom that began in 1946. About four million babies were born each year during the 1950s—almost 77 million babies in all by the time the boom finally tapered off in 1964. It was the largest generation in history—that is, until their children were born. The Millennial generation now outnumbers them.

Such a sudden increase in population swept everything before it: old ideas of work and living. This was accompanied by an unparalleled prosperity, something Americans had not seen since the hardships of the Great Depression and World War II.

The Baby Boom happened because Americans were confident that the future held nothing but peace and prosperity. Between 1945 and 1960, the gross national product more than doubled.

Much of this increase came from government spending: the construction of interstate highways and schools, the distribution of veterans' benefits and most of all the increase in military spending—on armaments for the Cold War and new technologies like computers. Rates of unemployment and inflation were low, and wages were high. Middle-class people had more money to spend than ever—and, because the variety and availability of consumer goods expanded along with the economy, they also wanted more things to buy.

Much of the growth was uncontrolled. Almost as soon as World War II ended, developers began buying land on the outskirts of cities and using mass production techniques to build modest, inexpensive tract houses. The G.I. Bill subsidized low-cost mortgages for returning soldiers, which meant that it was often cheaper to buy one of these suburban houses than it was to rent an apartment in the city.

There were undesirable consequences for older communities in decline. English philosopher Edmund Burke said that "traditional societies are organic wholes. If you disintegrate a society's physical setting, as [suburban] sprawl has done, you tend to disintegrate its culture as well."

The population boom also caused the air and water pollution that spawned the USEPA in the 1970s. Sociologist and historian Lewis Mumford catalogued this in his famous book *City In History*[1] where he argued that smart urban planning could mitigate the effects of urban sprawl by compacting the living

---

[1] Mumford, Lewis. *The city in history: Its origins, its transformations, and its prospects.* Vol. 67. Houghton Mifflin Harcourt, 1961.

areas, thus leaving more open space for recreation and agriculture to create more economically sustainable and environmentally friendly towns and cities.

The environmental movement also helped to create the idea of livable cities. In reaction to suburban sprawl, it brought back the idea of more traditionally planned cities that served families and communities first, rather than economic interests. It made sense to me that people would want more close-knit and well-functioning neighborhoods, especially for children needing a safe space to grow. Businesses should be integrated into those communities, rather than kept in separate zoning districts that required long commuting distances: another environmental consideration to mitigate air pollution caused by automobile commuting.

I and several others living in Santa Barbara and the Goleta Valley were interested in a more ecologically friendly and less auto-dependent community. Drs. Susanne Lennard, architect, and her husband, child psychologist Henry Lennard, were two disciples of "livable cities". They influenced our thinking.

The Lennards founded the Making Livable Cities organization in 1986. It began holding Livable Cities conferences, hosting mayors and urban planners from throughout the world.

In one of those conferences that I attended, the Dean of Urban Planning from Venice, Italy, extolled the virtues of pedestrian-friendly Venice and Venice's many public spaces that created its close-knit community. He even offered his listeners a personal tour of Venice, should we decide to visit him one day!

Mayors and planners from as far away as India, South America, and Singapore attended and presented papers—all wanting to show off their cities' people-friendly plans that had evolved over centuries of traditional living.

Central to their ideas was that communities had to be safe from crime, with sustainable economic growth that did little environmental damage. This was achieved by creating town centers built around squares, or plazas that became central community meeting places.

The Greeks and Romans had their public forums and amphitheaters that served their communities. Traditional European cities have open squares or plazas surrounded by shops and apartments from which families can watch their children while doing their own work.

The safety of children must be paramount. Its website, MakingCitiesLivable.org, states:

> To be sustainable, a neighborhood, town or city must **SUSTAIN ITS CHILDREN** [their emphasis]. It must provide a physical environment that ensures children's health, develops their faculties, and fosters their love for community, and for nature. In this way, children grow up to become agents of sustainability.

It is a messianic statement, but saving cities from themselves is a messianic endeavor. These conferences were tremendously exciting for those interested in building sustainable communities that combined good jobs with a human-scale environment. Dr.

Henry Lennard had developed the concept of child-centered communities where children are able to roam and explore their neighborhoods on their own. They could get to school without being ferried around by a soccer mom, or anyone in a car that prevented them from exploring their surroundings, creating a sense of autonomy and personal responsibility so important for success in later life.

Many Goleta residents were idealistic former UC Santa Barbara students opposed to anything that hinted at urban; that might disturb the largest Monarch Butterfly Preserve in the west coast, for example. Their vision had to be included in a community plan. Similarly, Goleta and the South Coast in general was becoming another Silicon Valley with major tech startups like Mentor and Citrix corporations located there.

Goleta had also been a major aerospace center in the 1970s and 1980s with Raytheon, General Motor's Delco and other defense contractors. UC Santa Barbara's technical expertise was nearby, as was Vandenberg Air Force Base where spy and weather satellites were launched into north-south polar trajectories.

How could we accommodate all this diversity in a well-functioning city?

Chapter Thirteen

Designing a New City Center

Many of us believed that a re-design of Old Town Goleta would be an ideal location to practice some of the precepts of True Urbanism, or Smart Planning, that could aid in the design for a new city. These were labels attached to what is now a worldwide movement.

The high crime rate in Old Town had been documented in the Redevelopment District Agency study. Environmental reports showed high traffic counts were causing air pollution, while successive floods following earlier drought periods required greater flood controls as well. We needed change.

We didn't realize at the time that California's Environmental Quality Act (CEQA) report would require flood improvements before anything could be done in Old Town.

The first step was to organize a design conference to provide design and planning alternatives for a new town center. We thought it obvious that without a community effort to create a community center with a unique identity that contrasted with neighboring Big Sister city Santa Barbara, Goleta's cityhood might never succeed.

The American Institute of Architects co-sponsored eight simultaneous Design Charrettes across the country and in Hawaii. According to Wikipedia, Design Charrette is an architectural term that describes a gathering of designers and interested parties to create an innovative atmosphere in which a diverse group of stakeholders can collaborate to "generate visions for the future". These weekend retreats brought professionals such as architects, designers, and urban planners together to envision and re-design a project area—such as a district or town center. All participants were interconnected via the Internet so we could report results to each other.

Design Charrettes originated with students of Paris's Ecole des Beaux Arts, France's major design school, in the 1800s. The students were used to cramming for exams at the last minute while riding in a charrette, or horse cart, to the exams. Our modern-day Design Charrette was an exciting chance for local students, environmentalists, and developers to participate in what might become a template for a future City of Goleta.

We assembled 100 design professionals and civic activists. It was a vehicle to begin the process of envisioning a future for the Goleta Valley community.

That weekend we "locked" ourselves into a large industrial building and broke into eight committees, each tasked to come up with a different design concept. The eight results covered the gamut of design ideas for Old Town, an area of no more than 20 city blocks and population of 5,000. Ideas ranged from a totally pedestrian environment accessible only to public transportation with room for pedestrian-oriented businesses and entertainment, to one that permitted automobile access, (which local business people badly wanted to sustain their businesses), but with more off-street parking and plenty of green landscaping.

Margaret Connell, a recent Goleta City Council member who supported the Old Town revitalization plan and wanted Old Town to be part of a new city center, voiced some of her concerns over the design problems:

> . . . So Goleta Old Town feels more embedded than the more recent housing and worksites, and it also suffers from some disadvantages of being "old." It lacks sidewalks through much of the older residential areas, though the city is taking steps to remedy this. There are many children who live here, but there are very few parks — a pocket park on Nectarine, a larger one on Armitos Avenue, and a four-acre, active-recreation park on Kellogg Street, which is still being developed.

The major environmental concerns were a lack of alternative transportation, such as buses and bike lanes, to manage traffic flow during peak rush hours and still service Old Town residents and businesses.

Flooding was also a major concern, despite periodic droughts. Santa Barbara and the South Coast had suffered several devastating floods during the 1990s that ended a prior 8-year drought.

The flood that broke the drought was called the March Miracle: in March 1991, 23 inches of rain fell, even flooding the Santa Barbara Municipal Airport and closing it for several days.

A second flood in 1995 caused another flooding of Old Town's main street. A three-foot deep stream of water from a torrential rainfall overflowed San Jose creek at one end of Old Town's boundaries. A climate scientist later said that the creek would no longer be adequate for containing flooding because the hard paved streets and roof surfaces in the surrounding neighborhoods had replaced the soil that had absorbed excess rainfall. Now the creek carried almost all of the rain's runoff.

Hence flood control improvements, such as an enlarged creek bed to carry the increased runoff, were required in the CEQA report as the first step in any redevelopment effort.

The droughts and consequential flooding also made everyone aware of the limited water supplies in California, as well as the potentially devastating drought/flood cycle. In fact, California's latest six-year drought ended with the greatest rainfall totals for Northern California since the 1880s.

Finally, Goleta achieved city status on February 1, 2002. It took four tries and a redrawing (several times) of city boundaries to gather in all of those who wanted to be part of the new city.

The work of the new City of Goleta has just begun. Its new community plan balances environmental with livable concerns, but there was another casualty of the Great Recession that caused an unexpected disruption of Goleta's future infrastructure upgrades, especially in Old Town.

133

California, to solve its own budget problems caused by the Great Recession, dissolved all 404 Redevelopment District Agencies in 2011, which removed the tax financing that Old Town was counting on to fix some of its housing problems and relieve the traffic congestion.

Has Goleta become a more livable city? Its residents think so, though affordable housing will continue to be a problem. Most of its growth has been to the west, carefully planned to preserve a more rural atmosphere with numerous bike paths and a new train station to provide more transportation choices.

The Livable Cities movement has evolved into a ranking contest as cities compete to attract the best and the brightest people, as well as jobs for them. The annual rankings of the most livable cities are touted by several well-known lifestyle publications and organizations, including the AARP Livability Index, Monocle's "Most Livable Cities Index", the Economist Intelligence Unit's "Global Livability Ranking", and "Mercer Quality of Living Survey".

Unfortunately, not a single U.S. city on the Economist's list makes the top 10 in a study of the world's 140 major cities. Melbourne, Australia, topped it in 2016, with Perth and Adelaide, Australia, also in the top ten. Honolulu, Hawaii, is the only American city mentioned at all. It makes the top ten list of most improved cities over the past 5 years.

It is safety of its residents and the threat of violence and terrorism that seems to have knocked American cities off the list and put Australia at the top of Most Livable Cities rankings.

How could Goleta solve the increasing dangers from violent extremism and domestic violence that make so many American cities unsafe?

Becoming a city enabled Goleta to contract with the County Sheriff to provide a neighborhood police service accountable solely to Goleta residents. It not only made Goleta safer for its residents, it was consequently listed as one of the 50 safest American cities in 2017, 15 years after its formation, according to a survey by Safewise, a security firm.

Goleta Old Town's revitalization is still a work in progress. Goleta gave up on the idea of putting a new City Hall in Old Town. It instead purchased a new City Hall to the west amid commercial office complexes. But the new City of Goleta has adopted the Livable City planning principles that we envisioned in the Old Town Design Charrette.

As a postscript to Goleta's story, I attended an event in 2019 that confirmed to me what a livable city meant to its residents. The City of Goleta Dam Dinner, a potluck dinner to which everyone contributed to celebrate their love of the city, was held on an earthen dam within the city limits that formed the small Lake Los Carneros. It was the "Love of the City" celebration.

The city described the celebration as "a free community dinner at the local dam where people brought picnics or bought dinner from food trucks and enjoyed their neighbors and the beautiful surroundings."

It was the fifth annual Dam Dinner, an event Goletans created in 2013 that was becoming increasingly popular among many cities wanting to honor their sense of community by making their city more lovable, as well as livable.

The happy faces of some 500 residents having a good time with friends and family while sitting side-by-side at tables strung along the length of the earthen dam was something to see.

It was evidence that the difficulties we encountered and obstacles we overcame to build such a community of happy people were worth it.

Chapter Fourteen

The Lessons Learned

I have found that successful community building at home or overseas has always been about addressing the deepest wants and needs of the members of that community, or country.

Given the chance, all people want to be in a "livable" community.

I experienced many ways to create livable communities, whether working in Turkey as a Peace Corps Volunteer, or with the USEPA in its early days striving to clean up the environment in its Western Region, or traveling with César Chávez as the UFW struggled to organize the farm working community to better their lives.

It was also possible to make my own community more livable for children and adults, with less crime and environmental degradation. The new city takes extreme pride in all it has accomplished to reach those goals.

I answered Kennedy's call because he made me believe that peaceful change was possible by working in communities that wanted to change for the better. The participants who desired change for the better soon realized that creating a more livable community that is safe for children is also safer for adults.

I also found that Dr. M. Scott Peck's principles, the community planning tenets of the Lennard's Livable Cities, or the union organizing methods used by César Chávez to form the UFW apply equally to making countries livable.

One of the most successful, worldwide organizations that I have continued with over the past 26 years offers even more service opportunities for ordinary citizens who want to make their world a better place. Rotary International is an organization with 1.2 million members in more than 190 countries that contribute to the betterment of their own communities.

Rotary is best known for its polio eradication efforts, but it also supports peace initiatives, including funding scholarships for young scholars studying for graduate degrees in peacemaking, and has supported grassroots development projects all over the world. The work of my own Rotary Club in the Eastern Democratic Republic of Congo helped to rebuild a valley devastated by its civil wars.

Rotary adopted the motto "Service above Self" in 1950, ten years before Sargent Shriver made it the Peace Corps credo.

It is a much larger version of U.S. Peace Corps, because the many projects that aid the poorest people at the grass roots level are administered by local Rotary Clubs, rather than directed by their governments.

And younger Millennial and Gen Z generations have been particularly active in movements that build a sustainable environment. A 2021 PEW research survey stated that

> While many forms of political engagement —such as voting—tend to be higher among older adults, 32% of Gen Zers and 28% of Millennials have taken at least one of four actions (donating money, contacting an elected official, volunteering or attending a rally) to help address climate change in the last year, compared with smaller shares of Gen X (23%) and Baby Boomer and older adults (21%).[1]

The Sunrise Movement is another national organization that asks for the direct involvement of younger generations in combating climate change with their 11 principles for creating a sustainable environment. Principle No. 2 states that

> We grow our power through talking to our communities. We talk to our neighbors, families, religious leaders, classmates, and teachers, in order to spread our word. Our strength and work is rooted in our local communities, and we are always growing in number.[2]

Principle No. 4 advocates non-violence, as did Martin Luther King, Jr. and César Chávez:

---

[1] https://www.pewresearch.org/science/2021/05/26/gen-z-millennials-stand-out- for-climate-change-activism-social-media-engagement-with-issue/
[2] https://www.sunrisemovement.org/principles/?ms=Sunrise%27sPrinciples

Remaining nonviolent allows us to win the hearts of the public and welcomes the most people to take part. We need maximum participation in order to achieve our goals.

We have just come through a multi-year coronavirus pandemic, as bad as the 1918 Spanish Flu pandemic that required years of recovery. The coronavirus pandemic has caused communities fragmented by the loss of jobs, rising poverty levels, and feelings of social injustice, to rebel in unpleasant ways by preventing change that would enhance their well-being.

Today's youth are answering the call to heal their communities as we did. According to a 2020 Deloitte Global Millennial Survey cited by *Forbes Magazine*, about three-quarters of Millennial and Gen Z respondents said the pandemic brought new issues to their attention and increased their sympathy for the needs of others in their local communities and across the globe. The same percentage said they plan to take real action to benefit their communities after the pandemic, while about 70% of respondents have already taken steps in this direction.[3]

They are in fact learning what we learned in earlier decades; most change for the good is a result of ultimately working at the grass roots level of communities.

I found that building a peaceful community is really about finding ways to bring people together. And once together, by meeting face-to-face in a physical space or via various public media, people soon recognize what it is they have in common.

---

[3] https://www.forbes.com/sites/deloitte/2020/09/16/millennials-and-gen-zs-are- shaping-a-better-world-for-us-all/?sh=ae80757c65cb

And by recognizing their commonality, they can find a way to solve their most difficult problems.

Now Cold War with Russia is looming because of Russia's invasion of the Ukraine. It brings back memories of President Kennedy and his New Frontier of possibilities that mobilized those in my generation to oppose wars and seek a peaceful coexistence.

How do communities that have been torn apart by all that has happened recover and talk to their neighbors with dissimilar beliefs? They must listen to their children, for they will want to leave their children a more peaceful, livable world.

ACKNOWLEDGEMENTS

These are some of the people, though not all, who helped me tell the stories of those I worked with to improve their communities. Thanks go to:

Leonard Tourney, novelist, teacher and editor, who read and commented on early chapters at the Santa Barbara Writers Conference, as well as other members of the SBWC workshops in which I read excerpts;

Returned Peace Corps Volunteers Jan Worth-Nelsen and Ted Nelsen for editing suggestions, and to Ted for sharing his story as a member of our Turkey V Rural Community Development Group;

Mike Miller, another member of Turkey V, for his description of the final days of the Peace Corps in Turkey;

Glenn Blumhorst, National Peace Corps Association President for comments on the Peace Corps chapters;

Dave Calkins, Chief, Region 9 Air Programs Division, former program administrator of the U.S. Clean Air Act, and member of the National Commission on Air Quality, for his comments on the early history of the U.S. Environmental Protection Agency;

142

Cousin John Gibson for sharing his memories of our time with César Chávez and the United Farmworkers Union, and cousin Robert Girling, Professor Emeritus, who sharpened my writing skills;

Michael Bennett, former mayor of Goleta, for his contributions to the history of the formation of the city of Goleta.

I also thank Marian Haley Biel and John Coyne, founders of the Peace Corps Writers Group, for encouraging me and other Peace Corps Volunteers to tell our stories of survival and hope living in the most primitive conditions.

Thanks to my professional editor Robyn Harrison for her terrific designing and editing skills.

I want above all to thank my loving and caring wife, Hendrika de Vries, whose own stunning memoir of surviving as a small child in Nazi-occupied Amsterdam during World War II provided me with an example of great writing and how it is possible to live under the worst of conditions. I would not be telling my story without her great heart and loving support.